Prosper Charles Alexander Haulleville, Henry Bellingham

Social Aspects of Catholicism and Protestantism

In Their Civil Bearing Upon Nations

Prosper Charles Alexander Haulleville, Henry Bellingham

Social Aspects of Catholicism and Protestantism
In Their Civil Bearing Upon Nations

ISBN/EAN: 9783744659826

Printed in Europe, USA, Canada, Australia, Japan

Cover: Foto ©Lupo / pixelio.de

More available books at **www.hansebooks.com**

SOCIAL ASPECTS OF CATHOLICISM

AND PROTESTANTISM

IN THEIR CIVIL BEARING UPON NATIONS,

TRANSLATED AND ADAPTED FROM THE FRENCH OF

M. LE BARON DE HAULLEVILLE.

BY

HENRY BELLINGHAM, M.A.,

BARRISTER-AT-LAW.

WITH A PREFACE BY

HIS EMINENCE CARDINAL MANNING,

ARCHBISHOP OF WESTMINSTER.

LONDON:
C. KEGAN PAUL & CO., 1, PATERNOSTER SQUARE.
1878.

[*The rights of translation and of reproduction are reserved.*]

AUTHORITIES CITED.

Lord Macaulay.
Saturday Review.
Hergenröther.
Quinet.
Vacherot.
Eugène Sue.
Cardinal Wiseman.
Very Rev. Dr. Newman.
Michelet.
Professor Poullet (Louvain).
Burke.
Lecky.
M. de Lavergne.
Hepworth Dixon.
Cardinal Manning.
Ranke.
M. John Lemoine.
Bergier.
Bayle.
Beza.
Rev. Dr. Leland.

BISHOP MILNER.
DE BRANDT.
COLLIER.
STOW.
NEAL.
PENN.
FROUDE.
HALLAM.
PRENDERGAST.
BLACKSTONE.
GRATTAN.
FREEMAN.
MENZEL.
LAING.
LINGARD.
COBBETT.
GUIZOT.
M. PREVOST PARADOL.
REV. S. R. MAITLAND, Librarian to Archbishop of Canterbury.
BAYARD TAYLOR.
DR. FORBES, Physician to Her Majesty.
GEIJER.
MOLESWORTH.
BARTHOLD.
ALLEN.
CARLYLE.
NIEBUHR.
BISHOP BURNET.
MONTESQUIEU.
INGLIS.
M. DE TOCQUEVILLE.
M. X. MARMIER.

PREFACE.

THE following pages contain a copious array of facts and arguments to refute the shallow but plausible fallacy against the Catholic faith derived from an alleged superiority in civilization attained by non-Catholic countries. This fallacy is plausible because it appeals to the lower and worldly notions of the day as to the nature of civilization. It is shallow, because it merely touches on the outside of the question. Nevertheless it has been repeated incessantly in this century, but chiefly in this country; and it belongs by especial right to the school of political economists, who for nearly a century have reduced all questions of civilization and progress to production, wealth, material development, which are supposed to constitute human progress.

The following facts are either studiously ignored or tacitly denied by this school of reasoners:—

1. That the highest standard of material progress ever known before the action of Christianity upon the world was that of Greece and of Rome. But neither Greece nor Rome can bear comparison with the moral progress of the Hebrew Commonwealth.

2. That the civilization of both Greece and Rome, in their legislation, their administration of justice, their public and their private morals, can bear no comparison with the laws, tribunals, patriotism, and domestic life of the Jewish people.

3. That the moral condition of Greece and Rome, both in their public and private life, exhibits a corruption so universal and so intense as to demonstrate the insufficiency of the lights and the laws of the natural order to create and to sustain the civilization of the human race.

4. That the civilization of which we are the offspring is not the civilization of the old Greek or Roman world, which was swept away before the germs of the civilization of Europe were planted.

5. That the civilization of Europe is the creation of Christianity; that the germs of our civilization are— (1) the Christian household created by the Sacrament

Preface.

of Christian marriage; (2) the Christian people formed by Christian education; and (3) the Christian State elevated by the higher law of Christian morals.

6. That the highest civilization, therefore, has a twofold foundation, material and moral, and a twofold progress, likewise both material and moral.

7. That the material foundation and progress which consists in the action and development of the reason and skill of men in arts, science, industry, wealth, and natural prosperity, as it existed before the moral foundation of a higher life and law was laid, so it may for a time survive the loss of that higher life. Great economical and material prosperity may be found, at least for a time, when the moral life of a people is declining, or even low. Material progress will continue after the moral progress has been checked, at least long enough to afford a plausible argument in favour of a non-Catholic as against a Catholic people, a province or a canton.

Such is, in fact, the fallacy of M. de Laveleye and his followers; and such is the argument which for a century has perplexed and deceived many minds.

The Baron de Haulleville has done good service, therefore, in treating of the future of Catholic nations. As Lord Bacon says, "Time destroys the fictions of men, but confirms the judgments of truth." Given time enough, and we see that the greatest material prosperity, unless supported by a higher principle, cannot endure; it carries in itself the principle of its own dissolution. Germany and France are direct examples of this truth. Mediæval Germany was a creation of Christianity. Modern Germany, since Luther, is already divided against itself. The northern half, which Comte placed as the lowest in the scale of European civilization, is precisely that half which has forfeited its Christianity. The southern half still lives on by the principle of its own creation. The material progress of France is greater than that of any country except our own. It is checked and endangered only in the measure of the decline of its moral progress; and its moral progress is checked only in the measure in which the infidel revolution of the last eighty years has checked it.

The master fallacy of the arch-impostor is the assertion that Christianity—that is, the Catholic faith and the Catholic Church—are the obstacles to civilization and progress. Christianity, as the chaos and corruption of the Greek and Roman world demonstrate, and as modern Europe shows, is the productive and the sustaining principle of all civilization, and of all progress in the higher culture of men and of nations. All things are preserved by the permanent action of the principle from which they spring. Christendom, or modern Europe, with all its civilization of national and international law, and with all the purities and sanctities of its domestic and private life, is the offspring of the Christian faith and of the Christian Church. European civilization will survive while it is Christian. If it ever cease to be Christian it will die out—not all at once, but stealthily, steadily, surely, under a fair countenance of seeming health. Its material progress will for a generation or two deceive many, till its moral progress has been turned backward, and its material progress has issued in the return of the Iron Age of universal armaments, mutual destruction, and the supremacy of might and matter over the moral laws of God and the higher civilization and onward progress of mankind. Donoso Cortes was mocked as a dreamer in his day, when he said, "Christian Europe is moribund. It is dying because it is poisoned. It cannot live by matter alone, and it is poisoned by every word that proceedeth out of the mouth of its philosophers." We are eyewitnesses of this dissolution. Materialists and doctrinaires, sceptics and Positivists, and the schoolmen of profit and loss, tare and tret, with their ignoble and unjoyous science, have dwarfed statesmen into politicians. These are the pontiffs and the prophets who are labouring to eliminate Christianity from civilization, and to make the nations conspire against the Catholic Church, the mother of their civilization, as the enemy of their welfare and the obstacle of their progress.

It is a sign of happy augury when we see laymen like Mr. Bellingham and the Baron de Haulleville devoting their intelligence and their industry to the refutation of this great deceit.

HENRY EDWARD,
CARD.-ARCHBISHOP OF WESTMINSTER.

April 12, 1878.

CONTENTS.

Page

CHAPTER I.
Neo-Protestantism of the Modern School of Continental Liberalism 1

CHAPTER II.
Causes of the Civil and Material Prosperity of Nations . 22

CHAPTER III.
Comparison between Catholic and Protestant Countries from an Economical point of view 69

CHAPTER IV.
Catholics and Colonization 108

CHAPTER V.
Catholicism and Civil Liberty 141

CHAPTER VI.
Catholic Countries and Education 181

Contents.

CHAPTER VII.

Relative Morality of Catholic and Protestant Countries . 215

CHAPTER VIII.

The Reformation in connection with the Development of Civil Liberties 232

CHAPTER IX.

Conclusion 279

CHAPTER I.

NEO-PROTESTANTISM OF THE MODERN SCHOOL OF CONTINENTAL LIBERALISM.

Opinion of Lord Macaulay on the perpetuity of the Catholic Church—Origin of this work—A new apologetic essay on Protestantism—Vague character of Neo-Protestantism—Its tactics against the Catholic Church—Result of Buckle's method applied to theology—Thesis of the modern school of Continental Liberalism *à priori* false—Aim and object of this work.

THIRTY years ago one of the most illustrious Protestant historians of this century wrote as follows:—

"How is it that Protestantism did so much and yet did no more? How is it that the Church of Rome, having lost a great part of Europe, not only ceased to lose, but actually regained nearly half of what she lost? It is certainly a most curious and important question; and on this question Professor Ranke has thrown far more light than any other person who has written on it. There is not, and there never was, on this earth a work of human policy so well deserving of examination as the Roman Catholic Church.

The history of that Church joins together the two great ages of human civilization. No other institution is left standing which carries the mind back to the times when the smoke of sacrifice rose from the Pantheon, and when camelopards and tigers bounded in the Flavian amphitheatre.

The proudest royal houses are but of yesterday when compared with the line of the Supreme Pontiffs.

That line we trace back in an unbroken series from the Pope who crowned Napoleon in the nineteenth century to the Pope who crowned Pepin in the eighth; and far beyond the time of Pepin the august dynasty extends, till it is lost in the twilight of fable.

The republic of Venice came next in antiquity. But the republic of Venice was modern when compared with the Papacy; and the republic of Venice is gone, and the Papacy remains. The Papacy remains, not in decay, not a mere antique, but full of life and youthful vigour.

The Catholic Church is still sending forth to the farthest ends of the world missionaries as zealous as those who landed in Kent with Augustine, and still confronting hostile kings with the same spirit with which she confronted Attila.

The number of her children is greater than in any former age.

Her acquisitions in the New World have more than compensated her for what she has lost in the Old.

Her spiritual ascendency extends over the vast countries which a century hence may not improbably contain a population as large as that which now inhabits Europe.

The members of her communion are certainly not fewer than a hundred and fifty millions; and it will be difficult to show that all the other Christian sects united amount to a hundred and twenty millions

Nor do we see any sign which indicates that the term of her long dominion is approaching.

She saw the commencement of all the governments and of all the ecclesiastical establishments that now exist in the world, and we feel no assurance that she is not destined to see the end of them all.

She was great and respected before the Saxon had set foot on Britain—before the Frank had passed the Rhine—when Grecian eloquence still flourished in Antioch—when idols were still worshipped in the temple of Mecca; and she may still exist in undiminished vigour when some traveller from New Zealand shall, in the midst of a vast solitude, take his stand on a broken arch of London Bridge to sketch the ruins of St. Paul's.

We often hear it said that the world is constantly becoming more and more enlightened, and that this enlightening must be favourable to Protestantism and unfavourable to Catholicism.

We wish that we could think so; but we see great reason to doubt whether this be a well-founded expectation.

We see that during the last two hundred and fifty years the human mind has been in the highest degree active; that it has made great advances in every branch of natural philosophy; that it has produced innumerable inventions tending to promote the convenience of life; that medicine, surgery, chemistry, engineering, have been very greatly improved, though not to so great an extent as the physical sciences.

Yet we can see that, during these two hundred and fifty years, Protestantism has made no conquests worth speaking of.

Nay, we believe that, as far as there has been a change, that change has, on the whole, been in favour of the Church of Rome.

We cannot, therefore, feel confident that the progress of knowledge will necessarily be fatal to a system which has, to say the least, stood its ground in spite of the immense progress made by the human race in knowledge since the days of Queen Elizabeth."

Who amongst our readers can have failed to recognize Lord Macaulay as the author of this remarkable quotation?[1]

Preserved from a spirit of bigotry by profound learning and good sense, he stands pre-eminent amongst English writers.

His name and that of Ranke suggested themselves to our mind when lately reading an article entitled "Protestantism and Catholicism Considered in their Bearing upon the Liberty and Prosperity of Nations," from the pen of M. de Laveleye, Professor of Political Economy in the State University of Liége.

The English translation of the original was prefaced by a letter from Mr. Gladstone, which according to the "Saturday Review"[2] did not add much merit to the work.

Herr Bluntschli, one of the Professors of the *Protestantenverein* or Prussian association of disunited Protestants, prefaced the German translation with a letter which suggests the idea of a man sure before-

---

[1] Critical and Historical Essays contributed to the "Edinburgh Review" by Lord Macaulay.

[2] "Saturday Review" of June, 1875.

hand of the approval of his readers; and M. de Savornin Lohnan did not hesitate to place this negation of the Catholic Church before his co-religionists in Holland.

Since, then, the question has been taken up by men of such repute, it may be well for us to consider briefly some of the arguments brought forward. We may begin by stating that the accusations made against the Church in the original article are as old as the Church itself, and have been frequently disseminated since the time of St. Augustine[1] and Julian the Apostate.[2] Theoretically the modern school of subjective rationalists recognize every religious belief, but in practice they do not extend their recognition to the Universal Church.

They hover like Milton's fallen angel over the waste of religious errors, throwing defiance at the sun, the light of the world, " O Sun, I hate thee."

We are informed by them that the Latin races are in a state of visible decline, and that the future of the world is in the hands of the Teuton and the Sclave ; that the French, Spaniards, Italians, in short all of

---

[1] *See* Klee's " History of Dogma," vol. i. p. 71.
[2] *See* Works of the Emperor Julian, published by E. Talbot. Paris, 1863.

Latin origin and blood, except perhaps those that combine something of a Genevan element *ex stirpe* Carteret, are degenerate; and that the Russians, the Prussians, and perhaps the Anglo-Saxons (though these latter are still too Catholic) are the nations now occupied in the resuscitation of the world.

The explanation of this phenomenon is, that all Latin races are afflicted with "*cupertinage*,"[1] according to the word used by M. Prevost Paradol.

The nations that neglect themselves are peopled with monks; all the Latin races except the liberals of Geneva have the Catholic virus in their veins.

Such are the reasons given to show that they are both physically and morally corrupt, and that they are therefore condemned to an incurable disease.

The Teutonic races, on the contrary, are chiefly Protestant, and since Protestantism alone possesses the words of eternal life and the promise of immortality, the races that are Protestant increase and prosper, and

---

[1] "Cupertinage" is a covert allusion to the office of St. Joseph of Cupertino, which was introduced into France with the Roman liturgy. A polemical discussion on this subject arose between men of letters, in which this word played a great part; and the cutting sarcasms of M. Louis Veuillot have become legendary in French journalism.

will continue to progress on the wings of purity and religion until the end of all things.

The Sclavonic races are mentioned with discretion; the present was not a suitable time to sing their praises.

In order that we may not be accused of distorting the ideas of the Liége professor we will content ourselves with an extract taken from the "Saturday Review."[1]

"This pamphlet has now been translated into English, with a preface by Mr. Gladstone.

The preface does not add much to the value of the composition, but it may serve the object it was probably designed to fulfil, and aid the circulation of the book in England. Even without his aid the work ought to please English readers, for it shows the immense superiority of Protestantism over its rival, and demonstrates how much more rich, free, happy, and prosperous are the adherents of the reformed than the adherents of the unreformed faith.

This to us is an old tale, but old tales are often true, and to most Englishmen it seems a proposition equally true and gratifying that all worldly and most spiritual advantages are on the side of Protestantism.

M. de Laveleye also points out that it is the peculiar evil of Catholicism that it corrupts its opponents and drives them into revolutionary despair. They seldom escape from the direct influence of the system in which they have been brought up, and are as positive they are right as ready to grind to pieces all who

---

[1] "Saturday Review" of June, 1875.

differ from them, and as ready to abuse power if they get it as any ecclesiastical faction.

They have nothing better to offer to the world than a bundle of negations and a general abhorrence of piety; and, as M. de Laveleye most justly observes, man cannot live without religion.

The general conclusion M. de Laveleye arrives at is a most melancholy one. The reader naturally thinks that all this laudation of Protestantism, this insistance on the necessity of a creed, must end in an exhortation to his countrymen to turn Protestants, but there is not a word of this in the pamphlet.

M. de Laveleye discusses the relative superiority of Protestantism and Catholicism, just as if he were discussing whether Mars or Venus was the larger planet. There was a time when many Catholic countries, and especially France, might have been Protestant, but the golden opportunity was allowed to slip by, and, as M. de Laveleye evidently thinks, cannot be regained.

Catholic countries are destined, he seems to consider, to be eternally the prey of alternate ecclesiastical and revolutionary despotism; but they are not destined to become Protestant. In short, they always believe too much or too little, and so Protestantism is not made for them.

Protestantism is thus a royal road to human happiness, which is closed to all except those whose princes happened to take a particular side in the sixteenth century.

There is much more of truth in this than Protestants have ever taken the trouble to recognize; but it is impossible to discuss how far it is a true theory, and why and what limitations are to be put upon it, without entering on theology.

In the sphere of politics, however, it must be admitted that a Belgian is much to be pitied who witnesses the fierce dissensions by which his country is torn, who sees even darker days coming, and who has also come to the mournful conclusion that the only way of escape that Belgians could have is barred to them by the blindness of their ancestors."

First of all, it is necessary to ascertain what species of Protestantism it is that these modern reformers advocate and approve.

Is it that of Henry VIII. or of Luther; is it that of Calvin, of Zwingle, or of Knox?

Is it Quaker or Puritan; Presbyterian, Congregational, Independent, Baptist, or Mormon?

Is the deity that they worship the god of Herr Sydow of Berlin, or, according to the language of M. Thiers, the "*bateleur*" god of M. Guizot?

Is the Christianity they recommend that of Dr. Colenso, or of Herr Bunsen; is it the Puritanical conception of the late Herr von Gerlach, or the sensational Puseyism of the Anglican school of thought; is it the liberal Protestantism of M. de Pressensé, or the Protestantized liberalism of Professor Bluntschli; is it the Calvinistic State-worship of M. Carteret, or the *Hegelian* Lutheranism of Prince Bismarck? M. de Laveleye has not informed us.

Such an omission may possibly constitute the cleverness of a diplomatist to the benefit of the public for whom he writes, but it reveals a doctrinal weakness that is easy to detect.

If it is sufficient to reject the principle of authority in order to be a Christian, or in other words, if one is only a real Christian when outside the fold of the Church, one Holy, Catholic, and Apostolic, it is necessary that we should ask for details, in order that we may become enlightened by a comparison of religious beliefs.

It is evident to all sensible minds, that the future cannot consist in a mere denial of the Catholic Church.

A public act of faith is necessary, and something definite and positive must be laid down.

We must ascertain whether M. de Laveleye's interpretation of the Bible brings him to profess the doctrine of the Incarnation, of the Word made flesh, of the Holy Trinity, the Resurrection of our Lord,— and in short whether it brings him to believe in the supernatural?

We must ascertain whether the followers of this new school consider prayer necessary, whether they are persuaded of the existence of the Devil, and so on *ad infinitum.*

The position they assume enables us to assert that upon all these great matters there is no certainty, and that if certainty did exist, they would not dare to admit it, for such an avowal would alienate many of their admirers and supporters.

In matters of religion, however, mere negation is insufficient; religion is not an abstraction, but a positive assertion—active, efficacious, and surrounded by an exterior form of worship.

Absolute certainty is necessary for assertion.

There is no doubt that subjective reason is able to attain to the philosophical conception of God, but there is need of revelation to define the living personal God of the Christian, and the entire region of the supernatural.

Instead of defending the Catholic Church against attacks which are in reality as old as the Church herself, it will not be difficult to take the offensive, and treat of the thesis laid down *à priori*.

Does Protestantism, in its thousand-and-one varied manifestations, from the established Churches of England and Sweden, down to the Socinianism and platonic Christianity of the modern continental liberals, in truth represent the doctrine of Jesus Christ?

If indeed each individual may freely interpret the sacred Scriptures for himself, there may logically exist as many different religions upon the earth as there are individuals—that is to say, a day may come when there will be no longer any religion at all.

The various Protestant communities carry within them elements that must eventually bring about the destruction of all Christian doctrine.

It was for this reason that statesmen like Quinet, philosophers like Vacherot, and poets like Eugène Sue, stated that the attempt to destroy Catholicism without putting anything in its place, did not and could not attain the end in view; and it was for this reason that they wished for the perversion of the Catholic masses to some form of Protestantism, so that they might become the accomplices of subjective rationalism in its warfare against the Universal Church.

M. de Laveleye in his pamphlet neither informed his readers what creed he eulogized, nor did he prove theologically that Protestantism in its general form, as the negation of the Universal Church, is the supreme and infallible expression of the Christian revelation.

He ingeniously conceals the barrenness of his positivist doctrines behind a convenient negation.

Scientific men do not ordinarily act in this manner, even when they have become the disciples of Buckle.

If we rightly understand the analysis that has been

made of the works of this writer, they are based upon the deductive method, and though we willingly admit it in the daily exercise of positive politics, we cannot accept such a principle in the logical foundation of philosophy.

M. de Laveleye applies it to the development of the subject of which we are treating, and puts forward an argument of refutation of invincible force: he lays down, with a certain boastfulness of tone, what he styles the benefits of Protestantism, and declares that they have produced a civilization in comparison with which the social influence of the Universal Church appears completely inferior. This style of argument, since it proves too much, in reality proves nothing. Athens in the time of Pericles, Carthage under the rule of Hannibal, Rome in the time of Virgil, and Spain under the Arabian caliphs have severally presented a spectacle of "civilization" which from the human point of view far excels in splendour the ponderous rule of Frederick I., twelfth elector of Brandenbourg and first king of Prussia, the violent *régime* of Gustavus Adolphus of Sweden, or the rough presidency of President Jackson in the United States of America.

According to this reasoning the paganism of the

Greeks, Romans, and Phœnicians, and the Mahometanism of the Arab races, would be infinitely superior to modern Protestantism. Herr von Hartmann[1] (the present fashionable light at Berlin) declares that "the inevitable result of the philosophical system of the *unbewussten* must be a return to paganism," and well may it be asked why such should not be the case? Where in the present day can be found such names as Æschylus, Euripides, Sophocles, Plato, Pindar, Aristophanes, Demosthenes, Phidias, and Praxiteles, such powerful orators, such sublime poets, such profound philosophers, and such gifted artists?

Where such magnificent conceptions as the Parthenon, Venus of Milo, or the Laocoon?

Has either the electorate of Brandenbourg, the town of Berne, the kingdom of Sweden, the territory of Washington, or the court of George I. of Hanover, ever presented a similar assemblage of poetry, of grace, of intellect, of beauty, or of natural reason?

Theophilus Gautier preferred Aspasia to all the Protestant matrons, and out of a hundred persons who will approve of M. de Laveleye's treatise, there

---

[1] "*Die Philosophie des Unbewussten*" (the school which is gaining the upper hand in Germany), by Herr Hartmann.

are not ten who would be of a different opinion to the wily pagan of Lutetia.

Is there one Protestant State that would not feel flattered at being compared to Rome in the time of the Cæsars? And yet no one could venture to assert that the Latins of Pagan Rome possessed this great political, literary, and economical superiority because they were not members of the Catholic Church.

We are unwilling to prolong this train of thought beyond bounds, but before bringing to a close this refutation *à priori*, let us suppose what does not exist, let us suppose that everything alleged to be true is actually true, that for instance in every case the different Protestant sects do display a striking superiority over Catholicism, and that the organic and fatal debility of Catholics in regard to politics, literature, and economy is precisely what it has been asserted to be.

Will anything even then have been theologically proved?

"Et quand l'autel brisé que la foule abandonné s'écroulerait sur moi !—temple que je chéris, temple où j'ai tant reçu, temple où j'ai tant appris, j'embrasserais encore ta dernière colonne, dussé-je être écrasé sous tes sacrés débris."[1]

[1] English translation :—
" And if the overthrown altar from which the people had fled

Men who aspire to enlighten the nations who have produced Charlemagne, Dante, St. Thomas of Aquin, Christopher Columbus, and St. Vincent de Paul, should not evince ignorance of the first rudiments of Christian doctrine. Our Lord Jesus Christ did not come down upon earth to give salvation to political societies, to enrich them, to teach them to read and write, to indoctrinate them with the principles of the free exchange of thought (excellent though such things might be), to lead them to discuss the properties of steam and electricity, or to develop in them a taste for literature. He was born in a stable, cradled in a manger, brought up in a workshop like any ordinary artisan, and crucified upon a tree for the salvation of mankind.

We shall spare our readers dissertation on such a subject; a glance at a biblical concordance will disclose any number of pages exactly to the point.

The essence of Catholic doctrine is summed up in the following words of Holy Writ: " Seek ye first the

---

were to fall upon me, even were I to find my death beneath its sacred ruins, I would yet embrace the last column of that temple which I love, and in which I have received and learned so much."

kingdom of God, and His justice, and all the rest shall be added unto you."

This "rest" has been given and will be given to all who are worthy of it.

The end, aim, and object of the Incarnation of our Blessed Lord is *supernatural.*

" Jesus Christ," such are the words of the catechism, "Jesus Christ came to deliver us from the slavery of the devil and eternal death." [1]

When the souls of individual citizens are saved, the empires they people are saved also, and as a simple matter of fact for the space of eighteen centuries no Catholic nation has become obliterated.

Nevertheless, even if a nation composed of faithful Catholics should become obliterated, or without being actually obliterated, were to vegetate without attaining to that pitch of success so dear to "men of the day," such a fact would prove nothing against the Catholic Church, since the Incarnation of the Word of God is beyond the order of nature.

St. Augustine, who lived in a society quite as civilized as that of our modern critics, and who was

[1] *See* St. Luke v. 31, 32; ix. 56; xix. 20; St. Matt. ix. 13; St. Mark ii. 17; St. John x. 10; xii. 46, 47, &c.; Epistle of St. Paul to Timothy, i. 15.

as learned in philosophy and civilization as any of the professors of modern Europe, wrote to a friend to console him for great worldly losses, words which have lived through centuries as a motto for all Catholics, "*Numquid Christianus es ut in hoc sæculo floreres?*" "Wert thou made a Christian in order to be successful in this world?" This quotation is the paraphrase of the text of St. Luke, "The children of this world are wiser in their generation than the children of light." [1]

If it were demonstrated with mathematical precision that the Catholics all over the surface of the globe were destitute of reason and intellect, and that Protestants were without exception consummate politicians, eminent economists, unparalleled writers, and that every one of them would become millionaires, theologically nothing would have been proved.

The possession and exercise of Christian truth, in its ideal purity and beauty, does not *ipso facto* bestow any equality of temporal advantages; a beggar may be a saint, but even a whole nation of saints would not necessarily possess any infallible promise of temporal bliss. Such a thesis is *à priori* false.

A man of intelligence and deep piety, a member of

[1] St. Luke xvi. 8.

the Institute of France, and a Professor of Political Economy, recently made the following remark: " Protestants and Liberals conceive a certain ideal of human society, and then easily prove that the States that are fashioned according to their conception, fulfil that ideal; when Catholics accept the ideal thus placed before them, they benevolently fall into the snare."

Another clever device of our opponents is to suppress in the most arbitrary manner all differences of nature, of latitudes, and of climate, all differences of custom and of national genius.

They would fain cast every individual in the same mould, which it is needless to say would be of their own pattern.

Such a conception of mankind is completely contradicted by facts; it would tend to render the whole universe a monotonous sojourn, and to reduce the human mind to a colourless and insipid uniformity.

Those who are cognizant of this error generally fall into another, by attempting to subject nations that are "ever-changing" to the tyranny of an exclusively logical rule, and offer to man as his earthly end and ambition, an inordinate desire for comfort and riches, as if the great end of life was luxury and ease, instead of its being but an apprenticeship of sacrifice and a preparation for death. Reflections like these are sufficient to undermine the whole collection of "deductive arguments" that have been brought against us, but modern works (not to mention those of ancient writers) like those of Auguste Nicholas, the Abbé Senac, the Abbé Martin, M. Charles Perin, Cardinal Deschamps, Manzoni, the Abbé Margotti, Hettinger, Klee, Moehler, Hergenröther, Balmez, Maguire, Dr. Newman, Cardinal Wiseman, and Cardinal Manning completely refute them.

We cannot admit the thesis that has been laid down, but we will nevertheless follow step by step the various evolutions that have been deduced, which course will be for us a demonstration *à posteriori*. Before, however, undertaking this task we may be permitted to warn the reader against any erroneous interpretation of our intentions; until we receive proof to the contrary we refuse to believe in this new-fangled form of Protestantism. We are personally acquainted with many pious Protestants for whom we have a profound respect; we believe in their honesty and sincerity of purpose, and we render homage to the excellence of their intentions and the uprightness of their private life.

If any such persons should read these pages, we trust

they may find in them nothing but a proof of our desire to serve faithfully the cause of truth, and should there be any expression capable of giving personal offence either to them or to the leaders of this modern school of liberals, we retract it beforehand.

We wish to put in practice the noble precept of St. Augustine, "*Interficite errores, diligite errantes.*"

CHAPTER II.

CAUSES OF THE CIVIL AND MATERIAL PROSPERITY OF NATIONS.

What is progress?—Is the phenomenon of the progress of Protestant nations the result of race?—The English Government the product of Catholic ages—Civil government of Catholic countries before the era of the French Revolution and the so-called Reformation—Civil strength and vigour of Spanish Catholics—Comparison between the civil liberty of the Italians and of the Prussians since the Reformation—Comparison between the social condition of the Irish and the Scotch—Catholicism in Switzerland.

E take the following passages from the commencement of M. de Laveleye's recent work :—

" Sectarian passions or anti-religious prejudice have been too often imported into the study of these questions. It is time that we should apply to it the method of observation and the scientific impartiality of the physiologist and the naturalist.

When the facts are once established, irrefragable conclusions will follow."

" The fact that Catholic races progress much less rapidly than those which are no longer Catholic, and that relatively to these latter they even seem to retrograde, appears to be proved both by history and more particularly by recent contemporary events.

This fact is so manifest that the French bishops make it a text of their reproaches to unbelieving Catholics."

The first conclusion is not very clear in its terms. In the first place, what is meant by the word "progress?"

It is a word that does not exist in the political language of the Anglo-Saxon race, and may be made to comprehend a great deal that is bad as well as a great deal that is good.

The English, the most practical people in Europe, never speak of progress; they turn their attention towards "improvement."

In the second place, what is meant by "retrogression?"

There must of necessity be an understanding as to the use of certain terms, and ours are the very opposite to those of the school of modern liberalism.

It is evident that M. de Laveleye has attempted to prove that all Catholic nations retrograde—that is to say, that they are a race of people who have no taste for political liberty.

Whence comes this phenomenon?

M. de Laveleye answers it as follows:—

"The English understand the parliamentary system and the exercise of practical liberty better than the French. Is this owing to the influence of blood? I do not think so; for until near the sixteenth century France, Spain, and Italy possessed provincial liberties of a very similar character to English liberties. The only notable difference was that the English had a single parliament and a centralized system which proved strong enough to hold its own against royalty. The Norman Conquest having united England, an united parliament was the result; and royalty being very powerful, nobles and commons combined to resist it, whereas elsewhere they were constantly at strife. The destinies of France and England only become entirely different from the beginning of the sixteenth century, when the Puritans had defeated the Stuarts, and when Louis XIV., by expelling the Protestants from France, had extirpated the last remnants of local autonomy and the sole important elements of resistance with which despotism might have been opposed."

Volumes might be written on such a subject, but we purpose to confine ourselves to a few brief considerations in reply to these summary assertions. Our adversaries admit that the great misfortune for France consists in the fact that it has been governed from the fourteenth century by the ideas of the Renaissance, and yet the Renaissance is in fact almost identical with modern continental liberalism.[1]

[1] An excellent article entitled "The Renaissance and Liberty,"

The tenets of the French Government at that period represented by royalty were fundamentally "liberal."

French unity is one of the principal results of a policy, which radical historians like Michelet, Quinet, Blanc, Esquiros, and H. Martin praise in a manner so compromising for the successors of St. Louis.

England had the good fortune to preserve all the political principles of the Catholic Middle Ages in her government, even after the troublous period of the Reformation; the best proof of which is, that she maintained an obstinate opposition to the introduction of the Roman code, whose royal Cæsarism overspread the whole continent of Europe from the period of the Renaissance. She preserved the text and principles of *Magna Charta*, a document having for its first signature the name of Stephen Langton, Cardinal of the Roman Church; she kept her old national traditions and ancient laws; and even to the present day points with pride to portions of her legislation dating back to the time of Alfred the Great; she maintained intact the interior organization of her secular government, and even in many respects the exterior form of the government of the Catholic Church.

may be found in the January number of the "Dublin Review" for 1878.

Since the Reformation the remarkable phenomenon exists of one nation who ceased to be Catholic (by what unworthy means is well known) but yet preserved an administration which has to this day remained the most Catholic in Europe, whilst another, who from the fact that the great mass of its members were Catholic deserved the title of Eldest Daughter of the Church, has never ceased from the time of Louis XVI. to be governed by princes and statesmen whose political doctrines are at variance with the teaching of the Catholic Church.

This fact of historical philosophy has been commented on with great power by M. Coquille, former editor of the "Univers" and now on the editorial staff of the "Monde." The glorious liberty of the institutions of England can never be thrown in the teeth of Catholics.

Those institutions are our own, the work of our Catholic forefathers, and worthy of the highest admiration.

To this very day the House of Commons is presided over by a person attired in the costume of the Middle Ages attended by his chaplain, who reads the prayers of Christians, just as in the days of Edward III. and Philippa of Hainault.

Close to the palace of Westminster is the tomb of St. Edward the Confessor and a grave-yard of the fourteenth century, which the piety of the English people has kept intact in the midst of a metropolis like London, but which would soon have been destroyed and converted into some practical use, if it had been in the hands of the modern continental school of progressists.

Representative government as it exists in England is the product of the Catholic Middle Ages; it has been lost in France since the time of Louis XI. (nearly a century before the official birth of Protestantism), and in the electorate of Brandenbourg, the principal Protestant Power of Europe, it can never be said to have existed at all.

It was preserved throughout the whole of the Netherlands, as well amongst the Calvinist population of the north as amongst the Catholic population of the south, until the reign of the "liberal" Joseph II. of Austria, and the "liberating" army of the French General Dumouriez, who deprived the entire country of its independence and secular liberties, by infecting the inhabitants with the false principles of the French Revolution.

The ecclesiastical principality of Liége, previous to

its overthrow in 1789, possessed a representative government very similar to that in England, which had existed for many centuries. Burke, in his "Thoughts on French Affairs," asserts that it is not easy to conceive governments more mild and indulgent than the Church sovereignties.

If any of our readers are interested in this subject we would suggest the works of M. Poulet, the eminent professor of Louvain, or those of the learned Canon Daris, to their notice.

It is a well-known historical fact that in Switzerland Catholicism and free institutions flourished for centuries in complete harmony until the era of Calvin, and that even after the troublous era of the Reformation the cantons which remained Catholic (equally with those that had become Protestant) preserved their Christian forms of democracy until their deliverance by the war of the Sonderbund.

Quite recently the hardy mountaineers of the Tyrol celebrated the fifth centenary of their local institutions.

Though it is the fashion amongst a certain class to sneer at this vigorous Alpine race, as men completely bound in the chains of Roman slavery, they have nought to covet from any nation in the world, either as regards nobility of mind, strength of body, or the

Material Prosperity of Nations. 29

possession of all the virtues that make men bold and free.

Can the constitution of St. Stephen of Hungary be considered inferior to the ancient institutions of England? Does anyone seriously imagine that because there were no Puritans or Quakers, Presbyterians or Independents in the various ecclesiastical electorates of the Holy Roman Empire, that therefore the people were less free and more corrupt than the half-civilized Scotch?

Would anyone have the presumption to assert that the peasants of Westphalia or the people of the Rhineland, wherein town and rural life is superabundantly vigorous, have become degenerate by reason of their profession of the Catholic faith?

Could it be said that Suabia and Franconia, lands hallowed and converted by St. Boniface, whose inhabitants preserved an amount of energy that manifested itself in the Thirty Years' War, in the Seven Years' War, and again under the rule of the French revolutionary authorities at the beginning of this century,— have nurtured people who have become degenerate by reason of the profession of Catholicism?

Is it not rather evident that their strong religious faith has alone preserved them powerful and pure, notwithstanding the legislation of liberal governments?

The example of Spain admirably illustrates our argument.

Since the time of Charles V. that country has been despoiled of the institutions which (for the sake of abbreviation) we shall style "the representative system;" the absolutism of Philip II. and of his successors, who were subjected to the influence of the Renaissance, the political absurdities of the Bourbons, and the liberal [1] doctrines of the present century, have all done their best to corrupt the Spanish nation.

Everything that could have been done has been done to effect the political destruction of a beautiful country inhabited by the most energetic race in Europe. Our argument is, that this people offered resistance, precisely because they were strongly attached to the Catholic Church.

For more than 700 years (the total existence of ancient Rome) the Catholic Goths of Spain, having taken refuge in the caverns of the Asturias, watched, prayed, and fought to preserve their own homes, and at the same time those of Europe, from the corroding

[1] Liberals, in Spanish, *liberales*. The word took its origin from the country of Cervantes.

contact of Islamism; their national assemblies were councils, and their laws, so deeply imbued with the spirit of religion that they were called by ecclesiastical names, were democratic in the Christian sense of the word.

For more than seven centuries this magnificent race of giants continued a struggle which in the end resulted in victory.

Scarcely, however, had they freed themselves by their undaunted courage from the yoke of the Mussulmans, than they were obliged for the space of three centuries to submit to the yoke of royal absolutism; and before long the last traces of their ancient institutions remained only in the mountainous district of Navarre.

But the Catholic faith was still cherished, like coals beneath the ashes.

At the beginning of this century Napoleon wishing to take possession of the country, used the following words: "Spain is a country of monks and priests, a country of cowards; I shall make an easy conquest of it."

History relates what took place: the Spanish people at that trying epoch of their national history proved themselves the worthy descendants of the conquerors of the Mussulmans; Catholic Spain inflicted the first mortal blow on the absolutism of Napoleon, at that time threatening the whole continent of Europe.

Since then the different shades of the liberal party who have held power, have reduced the country of Isabella the Catholic to its present condition.

The mass of the Catholic population have resisted in our day, and we have an intimate conviction that Spain, brought up and nurtured by the maternal hand of the Church, will become once more in its religious unity one of the first nations of the human race. Its literature excels that of every Protestant country in the world in depth, in moral riches, and æsthetic splendour; its painters and architects figure in the first rank in the Pantheon of artists; and it possesses a body of clergy whose bishops astounded the assembled Fathers at the Œcumenical Council of 1870 by their prodigious knowledge of science and theology. It possesses monuments which are like poems in stone; it has held the commerce of the entire universe in its power; it has spread humanity throughout half the world, and has alone founded more colonies than every other nation put together. Many persons allege that its present diminished power and grandeur is the result of its close alliance with the Church, but

Material Prosperity of Nations. 33

the assertion is an historical absurdity; it is the liberal party, with their self-complacent spirit of dictation and their enlightened following of socialists and atheists, who have momentarily arrested civil growth in a land so rich and fruitful, in the country of the Asturian Goths, of the Cid and the Romanceros, of Murillo, Velasquez, Lope de Vega, of Calderon and Cervantes, in the adopted country of Christopher Columbus and Fernando Cortez, in the land of the burial-place of Charles V., and the cradle of St. Ignatius and Balmez. We take the following quotation from an excellent work of this latter, entitled, "*El Protestantismo comparado con el Catolicismo,*"[1] "Protestantism and Catholicism compared together :"—

"We may expect much from the right instinct of the Spanish nation, from her proverbial gravity, which so many misfortunes have only augmented, and from that fact which teaches her so well how to discern the true path to happiness, by rendering her deaf to the insidious suggestions of those who seek to lead her astray. Although for so many years, owing to a fatal combination of circumstances and a want of harmony between the social and political order, Spain has not been able to obtain a government which understands her feelings and instincts, which follows her inclinations, and promotes her prosperity, we still cherish the hope that the day will come when from her own bosom, so

---

[1] This work has been translated into English under the title of "European Civilization." Published by Burns and Oates.

fertile in future life, will come forth the harmony which she seeks and the equilibrium which she has lost.

In the meantime it is of the highest importance that all men who have Spanish hearts in their breasts, and who do not wish to see the vitals of their country torn to pieces, should unite and act in concert to preserve her from the genius of evil.

Their unanimity will prevent the seeds of perpetual discord from being scattered on our soil—will ward off this additional calamity, and will preserve from destruction those precious germs whence may arise with renovated vigour our civilization, which has been so much injured by disastrous events.

The soul is overwhelmed with painful apprehensions at the thought that a day may come when religious unity will be banished from among us—that unity which is identified with our habits, our customs, our manners, our laws; which guarded the cradle of our monarchy in the cavern of Covadonga, and which was the emblem on our standard during a struggle of eight centuries against the formidable Crescent.

That unity which developed and illustrated our civilization in times of the greatest difficulty; that unity which followed our terrible *tercios*, when they imposed silence upon Europe; which led our sailors when they discovered the New World, and guided them when they for the first time made the circuit of the globe; that unity which sustains our soldiers in their most heroic exploits, and which, at a recent period, gave the climax to their many glorious deeds in the downfall of Napoleon.

You who condemn so rashly the work of ages, you who offer so many insults to the Spanish nation, and who treat as barbarism and ignorance the regulating principle of our civilization, do you know what it is you insult?

Do you know what inspired the genius of Gonsalva, of Ferdinando Cortez, of the conqueror of Lepanto?

Do not the shades of Garcilazo, of Herrera, of Ercilla, of

Fray Luis de Leon, of Cervantes, of Lope de Vega, inspire you with any respect? Can you venture to break the tie which connects us with them, to make us the unworthy posterity of these great men? Do you wish to place an impassable barrier between their faith and ours—between their manners and ours—to make us destroy all our traditions, and to forget our most inspiring recollections?

Do you wish to preserve the great and august monuments of our ancestors' piety among us only as a severe and eloquent reproach?

Will you consent to see dried up the most abundant fountains to which we can have recourse, to revive literature, to strengthen science, to reorganize legislation, to re-establish the spirit of nationality, to restore our glory, and replace this nation in the high position which her virtues merit, by restoring to her the peace and happiness which she seeks with so much toil, and which her heart is so sadly in need of?"

Catholic Spain may again be great and powerful when Lutheran Prussia shall have ceased to exist, or shall have been reduced to the original limits of the margravate of Brandenbourg.

Who can tell?[1] Herr Baumstark, a man of note, formerly a judge in the Grand Duchy of Baden, has written an interesting work[2] on Spain and the faults

[1] An old prophecy is extant in Germany that Prussia would develop to a wonderful extent, and would finally be reduced to her original limits.

[2] This work, originally published at Wurzburg, has been translated into French by the Baron de Lamerzau, under the title of "*Une excursion en Espagne.*" Toba, Paris, 1872, 1 vol. in 8vo.

committed by various bad governments in that country, from which the following is a quotation:—

"I have an intimate conviction that Spain, so far from approaching anything that would resemble a state of decline, is on the eve of a considerable and glorious development.

Even if the worst were to happen, if the torch of civil war were again to envelop the country in its flame—if the party of destruction and negation were to attain temporary power, such occurrences would not alter my convictions.

Events of this sort may be hard and cruel for the individuals who have to suffer as victims, but it is only in external appearance that they hinder the real increase of development.

The Spanish nation, endowed with an enormous amount of moral and intellectual power, as yet intact, has known, whilst adopting what is really good in the modern form of European civilization, how to preserve itself from the greater number of corruptions which flow from it elsewhere.

It is this national trait of character that makes me feel convinced that the future of this people will be great and brilliant, and that what is necessary will come to pass.

If anyone wishes to avail himself of the substance of the truths I have brought back from Spain, he will find them concentrated in the following propositions, which contain their quintessence:—

(1.) The Spanish government is not in a state of decline or degradation, but is, on the contrary, entirely occupied with its intellectual and material progress, and offers the most sanguine hopes of success.

(2.) The solid basis of this development, if it is to result in a durable prosperity, must continue to be Catholicism and the monarchical system.

Material Prosperity of Nations. 37

(3.) With regard to arts and literature, Spain can well bear comparison with any nation in the world.

(4.) As to ourselves, the children of central Europe, we might to our own advantage take lessons from the Spaniards, and should find ourselves in many points their inferiors."

In the year 1723 the population of Spain amounted to 7,625,000 souls; which number increased to 14,937,837 in the year 1857, to 15,151,677 in 1860, and to 16,732,052 in the year 1868. In 1850 the value of general commerce reached the sum of 1,150 millions of reals. In 1860 it had become 2,584 millions, and in the year 1867, 2,937 millions.

As regards the moral civilization of a nation, we do not attach a sovereign importance to statistics of this sort, but in contrast to the assertions of the liberals, they assume an eloquent significance. Until the period of the Renaissance the republics of the Peninsula were not politically inferior to England. From that epoch, which commenced sooner in Italy than elsewhere, they were subjected, it is true, to the pernicious influences of doctrines which are now called "liberal," and of which Machiavelli was one of the most celebrated theorists.

Religious manners and customs tempered to a great extent the fatal consequences of the system, but when one realizes the fact that the Popes of that period, in their capacity as temporal sovereigns, for a time encouraged and applauded it, one is the more constrained to admire the divine structure of the Church which has preserved incorruptible the deposit of the eternal promises.

A treatise[1] has been written on the cities and republics of Italy, in which the causes that led to the premature decline of free institutions have been investigated.

No one, we presume, would be so unreasonable as to deny that any improvement was effected by the Renaissance, or to disparage the works of Michael Angelo, but it may be as well to point out for the benefit of some of our readers, that many of the distinguished Latin artists of that period, who find favour in the eyes of modern liberals, were, though Catholics, imbued with much that was to be deplored in the exaggerated return to Pagan art.

There is little to admire in the various Italian governments that have existed since the Renaissance; the true Catholic ideal is neither the dictatorship of

---

[1] *See* "History of the Cities of Lombardy, from their origin until the end of the Thirteenth Century," by M. le Baron de Haulleville. Didier, Paris, 1857. 2 vols. in 8vo.

the Medicis, the mild liberalism of the Florentine House of Lorraine, nor the refined absolutism of the Neapolitan Bourbons.

Nevertheless, Italy, as a whole, was not less materially successful than Sweden or Prussia, whilst as regards the spiritual world, it shone with a splendour that no one can deny. The courts of Italy were undoubtedly superior in literary and artistic attainments to those of Stockholm, Copenhagen, Potsdam, and London. The patrimony of St. Peter, the civil territory of the Roman Church, the most ancient sovereignty of Europe, which was to Europe what Washington is to the American Confederation, preserved until the advent of a French army of "liberators" at the close of last century, a model type of *self-government*, which the anti-Catholic "civilization" of the nineteenth century has completely changed.[1]

From the fourteenth century until the arrival of French revolutionary troops in the year 1790, Romagna and Bologna were an oasis of political felicity in Europe. It is true that these places did not enjoy "liberty of worship" in the sense in which modern

---

[1] Burke speaks in high praise of the self-government in the Pontifical States during the reign of Pius VI. (Works, vol. v. p. 367.)

liberals understand the term, but will anyone presume to assert that "liberty of worship" was tolerated in Protestant countries such as Sweden, Prussia, or England, or that anyone was permitted to criticize the established churches in those countries?

Did there exist in anyone of them the least semblance of religious liberty?

Is it not well known that the only uncontested liberty was that of reviling and persecuting the Catholic Church?

In Prussia and in Sweden a species of religious tyranny prevailed, which was redundant with hypocrisy and brutality. In England, religious liberty only dates as far back as 1829, when Catholic emancipation was extorted from a reluctant government. Not many years ago a Catholic priest in the country of Lord Macaulay and Mr. Gladstone was unable to show himself in public without rendering himself liable to criminal penalties, and to this day the laws against the Jesuits have never been repealed. Unless, then, "civilization" consists in an entire negation of the Catholic Church, and unless there is no real truth in the principles of political liberty, Italy during the last few centuries cannot be considered as inferior to Protestant nations, but should rather take precedence of them.

Material Prosperity of Nations. 41

With this picture of the Catholic Spaniards and Italians on the one hand, and of Prussian, Swedish, and English Protestants on the other, let us simply ask the question, which of the two groups of nations most truly represent the noble and fruitful ideas that have occupied mankind since the passion and death of our Lord Jesus Christ?

We will only add the fact that from the period of the Protestant Reformation till the year 1848, the Prussian territory (the stronghold of Lutheran tenets) was the least "civilized" of all nations according to the ideas preconceived by the modern school of liberals, and that were it not for her splendid military achievements in 1866 against Austria, and in 1871 against France, the greater number of that school of thought would not admit without protest the exaggerated praises that have recently been bestowed upon her from various quarters.

A great deal has been said with reference to Ireland and Scotland, which, though plausible, will not bear investigation.

The following quotation is from the pen of M. de Laveleye :—

"It is admitted that the Scotch and Irish are of the same origin. Both have become subject to the English yoke. Until the sixteenth century Ireland was much more civilized than Scotland; and during the first part of the Middle Ages Ireland was a focus of civilization, whilst Scotland was still a den of barbarism. Since the Scotch have embraced the reformed religion, they have outrun even the English. The climate and the nature of the soil prevent Scotland from being as rich as England, but Macaulay proves that since the seventeenth century the Scotch have in every way surpassed the English.

Ireland, on the other hand, devoted to Ultramontanism, is poor, miserable, and agitated by the spirit of rebellion ; she seems incapable of raising herself by her own strength.

What a contrast, even in Ireland, between the exclusively Catholic Connaught and the province of Ulster, where Protestantism prevails! Ulster is enriched by industry, Connaught presents nought but a picture of desolation," &c. &c.

The idea of comparison has evidently been borrowed from Macaulay; but though that great writer takes the part of his fellow Protestants, he never allows himself to be carried away by sentiment, but writes with great reserve and fairness.

Thus he asserts that it is difficult to decide whether England owes most to the Catholic religion or to the Reformation.

The picture he draws of Ireland and Scotland at the death of Queen Elizabeth bears no resemblance whatever to the description of the same by M. de Laveleye, as the reader can judge for himself.

The following are his words :—

Material Prosperity of Nations. 43

"*In the year* 1603 *the great Queen died.* That year is on many accounts one of the most important epochs in our history. It was then that both Scotland and Ireland became parts of the same empire with England.

Both Scotland and Ireland, indeed, had been subjugated by the Plantagenets, but neither country had been patient under the yoke.

Scotland had, with heroic energy, vindicated her independence—had from the time of Robert Bruce been a separate kingdom, and was now joined to the southern part of the island in a manner which rather gratified than wounded her national pride.

Ireland had never, since the days of Henry II., been able to expel the foreign invaders, but she had struggled against them long and fiercely.

During the fourteenth and fifteenth centuries the English power in that island was constantly declining, and in the days of Henry VII. had sunk to the lowest point.

The Irish dominions of that prince consisted only of the counties of Dublin and Louth, of some parts of Meath and Kildare, and of a few sea-ports scattered along the coast. A large portion even of Leinster was not yet divided into counties.

Munster, Ulster, and Connaught were ruled by petty sovereigns, partly Celts and partly degenerate Normans, who had forgotten their origin and had adopted the Celtic language and manners. But during the sixteenth century the English power had made great progress. The half-savage chieftains who reigned beyond the pale had yielded one after another to the lieutenants of the Tudors. At length, a few weeks before the death of Elizabeth, the conquest, which had been begun more than four hundred years before by Strongbow, was completed by Mountjoy.

Scarcely had James I. mounted the English throne when the

last O'Donnell and O'Neill who have held the rank of independent princes kissed his hand at Whitehall. Thenceforward his writs ran, and his judges held assizes in every part of Ireland, and the English law superseded the customs which had prevailed among the aboriginal tribes.

In extent Scotland and Ireland were nearly equal to England, but were much less thickly peopled than England, and were very far behind her in wealth and civilization.

Scotland had been kept back by the sterility of her soil, and, in the midst of light, the thick darkness of the middle ages still rested on Ireland.

The population of Scotland, with the exception of the Celtic tribes, which were thinly scattered over the Hebrides and over the mountainous parts of the northern shires, was of the same blood with the population of England, and spoke a tongue which did not differ from the purest English more than the dialects of Somersetshire and Lancashire differed from each other.

In Ireland, on the contrary, the population, with the exception of the small English colony near the coast, was Celtic, and still kept the Celtic speech and manners.

In national courage and intelligence both the nations which now became connected with England ranked high.

In perseverance, in self-command, in forethought, in all the virtues which conduce to success in life, the Scots have never been surpassed.

The Irish, on the other hand, were distinguished by qualities which tend to make men interesting rather than prosperous. They were an ardent and impetuous race, easily moved to tears or laughter, to fury or to love.

Alone among the nations of northern Europe they had the susceptibility, the vivacity, the .natural turn for acting and rhetoric, which are indigenous on the shores of the Mediterranean Sea.

In mental culture Scotland had an indisputable superiority.

Though that kingdom was then the poorest in Christendom, it already vied in every branch of learning with the most favoured countries.

Scotsmen, whose dwellings and whose food were as wretched as those of the Icelanders of our day, wrote Latin verse with more than the delicacy of Vida, and made discoveries in science which would have added to the renown of Galileo. Ireland could boast of no Buchanan or Napier.

The genius with which her aboriginal inhabitants were largely endowed showed itself as yet only in ballads, which, wild and rugged as they were, seemed to the judging eye of Spenser to contain a portion of the pure gold of poetry.

Scotland, in becoming part of the British monarchy, preserved all her dignity. Having during many generations courageously withstood the English arms, she was now joined to her stronger neighbour on the most honourable terms.

She gave a king instead of receiving one. She retained her own constitution and laws.

Her tribunals and parliaments remained entirely independent of the tribunals and parliaments which sat at Westminster. The administration of Scotland was in Scottish hands, for no Englishman had any motive to emigrate northward, and to contend with the shrewdest and most pertinacious of all races for what was to be scraped together in the poorest of all treasuries.

Meanwhile Scottish adventurers poured southwards, and obtained in all the walks of life a prosperity which excited much envy, but which was in general only the just reward of prudence and industry.

Nevertheless, Scotland by no means escaped the fate ordained for every country which is connected but not incorporated with another country of greater resources. Though in name an independent kingdom, she was, during more than a century, really treated in many respects as a subject province.

Ireland was undisguisedly governed as a dependency won by the sword. Her rude national institutions had perished.

The English colonists submitted to the dictation of the mother country, without whose support they could not exist, and indemnified themselves by trampling on the people among whom they had settled.

The parliaments which met at Dublin could pass no law which had not previously been approved by the English Privy Council.

The authority of the English legislature extended over Ireland.

The executive administration was intrusted to men taken either from England or from the English pale, and in either case regarded as foreigners, and even as enemies, by the Celtic population.

But the circumstance which more than any other has made Ireland to differ from Scotland remains to be noticed.

Scotland was Protestant.

In no part of Europe had the movement of the popular mind against the Roman Catholic Church been so rapid and violent.

The reformers had vanquished, deposed, and imprisoned their idolatrous sovereign. They would not endure even such a compromise as had been effected in England.

They had established the Calvinistic doctrine, discipline, and worship, and they made little distinction between popery and prelacy, between the Mass and the Book of Common Prayer.

Unfortunately for Scotland, the prince whom she sent to govern a fairer inheritance had been so much annoyed by the pertinacity with which her theologians had asserted against him the privileges of the synod and the pulpit, that he hated the ecclesiastical polity to which she was fondly attached as much as it was in his effeminate nature to hate anything, and had no sooner mounted the English throne than he began to show an intolerant zeal for the government and ritual of the English Church.

The Irish were the only people of northern Europe who had remained true to the old religion.

This is to be partly ascribed to the circumstance that they were some centuries behind their neighbours in knowledge.

But other causes had co-operated.

The Reformation had been a national as well as a moral revolt.

It had been not only an insurrection of the laity against the clergy, but also an insurrection of all the branches of the great German race against an alien domination.

It is a most significant circumstance that no large society of which the tongue is not Teutonic has ever turned Protestant, and that wherever a language derived from that of ancient Rome is spoken, the religion of modern Rome to this day prevails.

The patriotism of the Irish had taken a peculiar direction.

The object of their animosity was not Rome, but England, and they had especial reason to abhor those English sovereigns who had been the chiefs of the great schism, Henry the Eighth and Elizabeth.

During the vain struggle which two generations of Milesian princes maintained against the Tudors, religious enthusiasm and national enthusiasm became inseparably blended in the minds of the vanquished race.

The new feud of Protestant and Papist inflamed the old feud of Saxon and Celt.

The English conquerors meanwhile neglected all legitimate means of conversion.

No care was taken to provide the vanquished nation with instructors capable of making themselves understood.

No translation of the Bible was put forth in the Erse language.

The government contented itself with setting up a vast hierarchy of Protestant archbishops, bishops, and rectors, who did nothing, and who for doing nothing were paid out of the spoils of a Church loved and revered by the great body of the people."

Macaulay has by this style of writing demolished more than one attack that has been directed against the Catholic Church.

As regards historical facts, the infamies perpetrated on the heroic people of Ireland for the space of 300 years under "Protestant civilization" have been frequently exposed by Protestant Englishmen who look back with shame and disgust[1] on the proceedings of their ancestors. Many excellent works on Irish history were published in the year 1875, in connection with the celebration of the O'Connell centenary in Dublin,[2] which throw floods of light on the sufferings of the people.

The Bill for the Emancipation of Catholics throughout Great Britain dates from the year 1829; O'Connell was the first Catholic who sat in the House of Commons at Westminster, and the first Catholic Lord Mayor of Dublin.

---

[1] *See* Lecky's "Leaders of Public Opinion in Ireland," page 124. Longmans, London.

[2] "History of Ireland," "Life of the Liberator," &c., by Miss Cusack, and others.

Before that time every government that held power in England, whether that of the Tudors, the Stuarts, Cromwell, the Puritans, the House of Orange or that of Hanover, may be said to have striven to emulate the other in brutality and cruelty towards the Irish; the motto of many of them being not only oppression and confiscation of goods, but complete extermination of the population. Cromwell and his unblemished Puritans made themselves particularly remarkable in the work of "civilization," but it will be sufficient for our purpose to recite a few historical facts relating to Ireland.

Elizabeth the Virgin Queen confiscated 600,000 acres, and James I. 2,000,000 acres of Irish soil; the government of the latter also caused a return of landed property in Ireland to be drawn up, to prove that nearly the whole of the country was in actual possession of the Crown, and that Connaught should be held as a fief of the Crown.

Steps of a similar character were taken under Charles I., and the Irish people know with what success. The Cromwellian army of "saints" perpetrated such horrible atrocities throughout the entire country that the remembrance of the maledictions of the sufferers is still extant among the people. The Catholics who escaped massacre were sent to America, or driven into Connaught. "To Connaught or to Hell," such was the language used by these founders of Protestant "*civilization.*"

Under the reign of William of Orange the Irish Catholics retained possession of no more than the tenth part of their soil.

From the downfall of the Stuarts the actual system of tyrannical oppression and cruelty was abandoned, to give place to the work of lawyers. Hypocrisy built up a monument of injustice which drew the following cry of indignation from the Protestant historian Gervinus ("*Geschichte des XIXten Jahrhundert,*" vol. vii. p. 438) :—

"A system of oppression opposed to all that is natural was invented, the plan of which was to impoverish and barbarize the masses of the people, in exterminating either the Catholic Church or the actual Catholic population itself."

In the years 1663 and 1666 the Irish people were forbidden to export their cattle, because their agriculture was considered to be improving, and in 1699 the exportation of wool was prohibited, because these unfortunate people were beginning to rival the English in this branch of trade.

No "papist" could hold any office under the State,

or acquire landed property; no papist employer could have more than two apprentices, for fear that Irish industry should gain too much power.

The English government, in order to impoverish Ireland as much as possible, imposed upon Catholics the obligation of an equal division of property amongst the children—a system practised, since the revolution of 1798, in France and Belgium, but one that has never been admitted in England or the United States of America.

Burke declared that it was a system calculated to ruin the small families, without their possessing the means to recover themselves by industry and intellect, since they were prohibited from retaining any kind of property, and according to him the whole code of Protestant despotism was so well organized to oppress the people and disfigure even human nature itself, that nothing equal to it was ever invented by the most consummate hypocrisy.

Until the reign of George III. Catholics were forbidden to erect schools, and the parents of the great Daniel O'Connell were obliged to send their son to Liége and Douai in order to find a Catholic school in which instruction might be given to the future liberator of their country.

It was only in this reign that the law was abolished which prohibited an Irishman from keeping a horse exceeding the value of £5 in his possession.[1]

The entire body of the Protestant clergy opposed Catholic Emancipation with the greatest vigour.[2]

Although some partial concessions had been made to the Catholics by the Irish Parliament at the close of last century, the feeling was strong against admitting them to equal rights with their Protestant countrymen, which showed itself in the fact that the corporations of the principal cities of an essentially Catholic country were almost exclusively governed by Protestants. Mr. Lecky declares that for forty-seven years after Catholics had been made eligible, not one was elected into the corporation of Dublin.

Here we have enough to prove the paramount injustice of the criticisms of the modern liberals. Are we not right when we accuse them of allowing themselves to be carried away by religious prejudice, when they make the amazing statement that it was the Catholic Church that rendered Ireland miserable,

---

[1] *See* Lecky's " Leaders of Public Opinion in Ireland." Longmans, London.

[2] Mullala's " Irish Affairs," vol. ii.

Material Prosperity of Nations.

and that it was Protestantism that had made England great and powerful ?

We cite the following page of history from "Le Français" of Paris as the testimony of an outsider to Protestant civilization in Ireland : [1]—

"In the year 1828 O'Connell considered the moment for action on the part of the Irish Catholics had arrived.

The question at stake was that of obtaining for Catholics the right of a seat in the House of Commons, and the right to occupy political and civil posts.

O'Connell determined to present himself to the electors of the County Clare, in order to force open the doors of that parliament which had hitherto been so obstinately kept closed.

At first sight it might appear that nothing would be easier than his return by the electors of the county, since the great majority of the people were Catholics, although the difficulty of admission into the House of Commons might be great ; but it must be borne in mind that at that period only those who paid a certain fixed amount of taxes had the right of exercising a vote, and that nearly all persons of this class were Protestants.

The only Catholic electors were the tenants and small farmers, who were completely at the mercy of their Protestant landlords.

The tenants had no natural inherent rights in the soil ; the whim of the landlord, or rather of his agent (as the landlord in most cases did not reside in the country), was of itself sufficient for their eviction.

Eviction, be it clearly understood, implied ruin. The tenant received no indemnity for the improvements he made. He originally received a piece of bare ground, on which he had to build himself a house, and the day of his expulsion saw him,

---

[1] "*Le Français*" of the 3rd August, 1875.

therefore, severed from his home. This was the work of the terrible crow-bar brigade.

Nothing is more heartrending or deplorable than the history of these evictions.

Irishmen and Irishwomen have more than once evinced in such cases a patience, the secret of which can alone be found in their strong religious faith.

Let us give an instance of what we mean. An old couple brutally driven away from their cabin were lamenting their forlorn condition.

'Ah!' said the old woman, 'here I am at the age of seventy-four years left without a shelter in the world; I who have never done anyone any ill, and who have often given hospitality to others. What have I done to be treated in this way?' 'Hold your peace,' said the old man. 'Hold your peace. Our blessed Lord suffered more than that in His Passion.'

Evictions were by no means isolated or extraordinary occurrences.

In the space of ten years, from 1841 to 1851, 282,000 houses were in this way destroyed. In 1849 more than 50,000 families were driven away.

It is impossible to travel over certain parts of Ireland without meeting at every step traces of ruins.

The excesses were so great that an Englishman and a Protestant (Mr. Bright) was able to say, '*It is impossible in travelling through certain districts of Ireland not to feel that enormous crimes have been committed by the various governments to which the country has been subjected.*'

It will be seen, then, how difficult was the situation of the Catholic electors in regard to their Protestant landlords.

Every vote for a Catholic (and the vote was not given secretly) brought with it *eviction* as an inevitable consequence; that is to say, ruin, and perhaps death.

Material Prosperity of Nations. 55

Until the foundation of the great Catholic association the farmer used to vote entirely at the will of his landlord. After the formation of the association, feeling himself supported and encouraged, his patriotism became inflamed, and he was inspired with veritable acts of heroism. What else but heroism can we call the conduct of a poor peasant, the father of a large family, in prison for a few debts contracted towards his landlord, who acted as follows when he was promised freedom, provided he voted against O'Connell:—

A struggle ensues in his breast, since he sees on the one side his country, and on the other his family dependent on him for their daily food. He accepts the bargain, and goes to the polling booth with faltering step and heavy brow. His wife in the crowd sees him, and divining what has happened throws herself upon him, and forgetful of her starving children piteously asking for bread, exclaims, '*Wretched man! what are you doing? Remember your soul and your country's liberty.*' The peasant understands his wife's language, votes for O'Connell, and returns to prison.

When O'Connell announced his intention of presenting himself as candidate for the county of Clare, the excitement in Ireland was intense. Preparations were made on both sides for a battle which each party felt must be decisive. On the one side was the government, the army, the wealthy landed proprietors; on the other a multitude of peasants (many of them in rags), the Catholic clergy, and the newly-formed association of O'Connell.

The battle was sharp and decisive, and the Protestant party soon perceived they were completely beaten. All the tenantry abandoned their landlords and voted for O'Connell, notwithstanding every threat of eviction or punishment.

The agitator was elected by an overwhelming majority, and, surrounded by 60,000 men, carrying aloft large branches in token of triumph, gave vent to the following cry of victory:—

'The men of Clare know that the only basis of liberty is religion; they have triumphed because the voice they raised on behalf of their country had first raised itself in prayer to God. Songs of liberty may now make themselves heard throughout our country, whose sound will travel through hill and valley with voice of thunder, and be wafted along the course of the rivers and streams, proclaiming far and wide that Ireland at length is free!'"

The Duke of Wellington used the following language from his seat in the House of Lords concerning the Irish shortly before Catholic Emancipation :—

"It is known to your lordships that at least half of the troops I commanded in the various campaigns undertaken for the security and independence of our country were composed of Roman Catholics. In recalling this fact I am persuaded that every other argument in their favour will be superfluous.

We must all recognize that without the blood of the Irish Catholics, and without their courage, we could not have gained our brilliant victories."

Connaught, which produced the celebrated Father Mathew, one of the great men of this century, is not in such a miserable condition as is represented; for instance, crimes against property are proportionately to its population less numerous than in Ulster.

The relative poverty of Connaught is almost exclusively the result of English misrule and tyranny.

Protestants are the last people who should presume to talk of the poverty or misery of the Irish peasants.

Material Prosperity of Nations. 57

What would be thought of a Turkish Pasha reproaching the Sclaves subject to the dominion of Turkey with their poverty, whilst the Turks themselves were living in ease and affluence?

What of the Russians reproaching the Poles subject to the dominion of the Czar, with their state of destitution, when the Russians themselves were indulging in every luxury and excess?

What of a judge upbraiding a man who had been robbed, with the condition in which the robber had left him?

The relative well-being of Ulster is the fruit of an execrable amount of violence.

The plan of the plantation was agreed upon in 1609. It was the old plan attempted before, though with less show of legality. The simple object was to expel the natives and extirpate the Catholic religion. The Protestant University of Dublin obtained 3,000 acres in Ulster, and 400,000 acres of tillage land were partitioned out between English and Scotch proprietors.

A Presbyterian minister, whose father was one of the planters, thus describes[1] the men who came to

[1] MS. History by Rev. A. Stuart, quoted in Reid's "History of the Presbyterian Church," vol. i. p. 96.

establish English rule and root out Popery: "From Scotland came many and from England not a few, yet all of them generally the scum of both nations, who from debt, or making and fleeing from justice or seeking shelter, came hither, hoping to be without fear of man's justice, in a land where there was nothing or but little as yet of the fear of God . . . . Most of the people are void of all godliness . . . . on all hands atheism increases and disregard of God; iniquity abounds, with contention, fighting, murder, and adultery."

The natives were forcibly expelled from their homes, deprived of their wealth, and treated with every indignity. The impious soldiery pursued the defenceless priests by night and day throughout the province, whilst they entered private houses at discretion and executed whom they pleased. The Bishop of Down and Connor was executed in Dublin by an English culprit under sentence of death, the only person who could be found to do the bloody deed.

The men whose lives the Irish people have always held more sacred than those of their ancient chiefs, were daily slaughtered before their eyes, and cruelties were perpetrated that would have excited the indignation of the heathen.

We shall refer, however, to Ulster in another part of this work.

M. de Laveleye asserts that "since the Scotch adopted the Reformation, they have surpassed in civilization and wealth the English themselves." If the English have been themselves therefore distanced by the Scotch, it is evident that the Reformation cannot be the cause of their progress, unless he means to assert that the English nation is still too Catholic, and that "*progress*" is only obtained in the direct ratio of the removal of a people from a positive basis of Christianity.

The writer should also inform us to which Reformation he alludes, for Scotland of all countries, with the exception, perhaps, of the United States of America, is the one most broken up and divided by religious factions.

We shall have occasion later on to mention Scotch Calvinism, and shall then speak of the shameful despotism which the sectarian spirit inflicted on Scotland from the era of the Reformation; for the present we will merely state the fact that there is no religious absurdity that has not found some adherents and supporters in the country north of the Tweed.

Will anyone undertake to show us what is the

analogy between this sort of anarchy and the material prosperity of Scotland?

That Scotland presents a picture of wealth and industry cannot be denied, but are there no other countries similar in character?

What shall we say of the inhabitants of the Ardennes? the peasants of the Campine, and the agriculturists of the sandy plains of Flanders?

The Liége professor, who has shown in his writings an appreciation of the rural economy of his own country, is perfectly justified in bearing testimony to the prosperity of the Scotch, but there is no need to give them more credit than they deserve. The fact that the Duke of Sutherland every year reclaims a certain number of acres of fertile ground from a barren soil can no more be attributed to the excellence of Protestantism than the agriculturist wonders achieved by means of Belgian State funds in the fields of Beverloo[1] can be attributed to the Catholic Church.

If the present prosperity of Scotland is to be regarded as the fruit of the Reformation, it has been very tardy in its growth. In this case also the present prosperity of Belgium should be regarded as the fruit

[1] Beverloo is a permanent military camp established in the middle of the sandy plains of Limbourg, in Belgium.

Material Prosperity of Nations. 61

of Catholicism, but such a line of argument is absurd and proves nothing.

The following passage from the pen of M. de Lavergne[1] is so excellent that we quote it *in extenso* :—

"Scotland is one of the principal examples extant of what may be accomplished by the power of man over nature.

Switzerland does not present such great obstacles to human industry, and Holland can scarcely rival it. The marvel of this development of prosperity upon a barren soil consists principally in the fact that it is quite recent.

Scotland has not the same antecedents as England. Only a century ago it was one of the poorest and the least civilized of European nations, and the last traces of its former poverty still linger in some parts, though on the whole it may justly be asserted that there is no tract of land under the sun so well organized.

Its products have increased tenfold since the beginning of this century.

The Scotch farmers, who were a hundred years ago almost without exception very poor and miserable, have not as yet realized such vast capital as their English brethren.

The population of the counties of Lanark and Renfrew, the chief seats of manufacturing and commercial activity, has increased in a hundred years from 100,000 to 600,000 persons, and that of the single town of Glasgow from 20,000 to nearly 400,000.

The seed of all these riches did not exist in the year 1750, but English gold, aided by the laborious and frugal genius of the Scotch people, has produced them.

As long as Scotland remained separate from England and

See "*Éssai sur l'Économie rurale de l'Angleterre, de l'Écosse et de l'Irlande.*" M. de Lavergne, Paris.

dependent only on its own strength, it vegetated, but as soon as it opened its arms to the funded wealth of its powerful neighbour, it developed itself to an extraordinary degree.

The most beautiful present that England made to Scotland was this union of the two countries, inasmuch as it comprised her constitution and political spirit.

Up to the year 1750 Scotland was the stronghold of the ancient feudal system; it only began to open its eyes after the battle of Culloden; and so recently as the end of last century, Ayrshire, which is adjacent to Galloway, was in a most deplorable condition of poverty and degradation," &c.

We are assured that Scotland owes its prosperity to its Protestantism, but as a matter of fact, until the battle of Culloden, in 1746, the Highland chiefs thought of nothing but the increase in number of their soldiers or retainers, attaching great importance to the strength of the armed forces they could muster under their banner.

Long after the social and agricultural condition of affairs of the Middle Ages had elsewhere ceased to exist, it still maintained itself in these retreats.

After the expulsion of the Stuarts the face of everything changed, and the cause and reason of this change forms an interesting and instructive study. The population, in part Catholic (for a certain portion of the Highlanders have remained to this day faithful to the Catholic Church), was too dense for the productive qualities of the soil. The chiefs of the various clans arrived by degrees at the conviction that they could get nothing from their mountains but by *exterminating* the inhabitants that resided on them, and from this time forth they began, first by covert and indirect means, and afterwards openly by the use of force, to decimate the populations their forefathers had multiplied for purposes of warfare.

The English government encouraged the undertaking with much diplomatic skill and foresight. Until the commencement of this century the landed proprietors executed these measures with some sort of appreciation for the feelings of their poor dependents, but since then the chief of the clan has generally forced his people to evacuate their dwellings.

A large proportion of these unfortunate creatures emigrated to America, others sought a home in the Lowland districts, whilst large sheep-farms were established upon the smoking ruins of their former dwellings.

In the year 1808 Lord Selkirk publicly set forth the theory of depopulation, which was styled *clearing an estate.*

This was the era when Sir Walter Scott lived

and sang the liberties and freedom of the Scottish people!

On one well-known estate in Sutherland the Highlanders were summarily ordered to quit their mountains and come and settle as sailors, fishermen, or ordinary agricultural labourers on that portion of the estate which bordered on the sea.

Those who refused compliance were forced to emigrate, and in this way between the years 1810 and 1820, 3,000 families were turned adrift, and deprived of lands on which their ancestors had lived.

If any resistance was offered the houses were burnt down or otherwise destroyed. These proceedings enabled 118,000 Cheviots and 13,000 head of cattle to graze on the hills of Sutherland, 415,000 pounds of wool were sold to the weavers of York, 30,000 sheep were delivered to the Northumberland farmers for slaughter, and the agent was made a Member of Parliament.

Our opponents are fond of asserting that the Latin cantons of Neufchatel, of Vaud, and of Geneva, because they are Protestant, excel in education, literature, art, industry, commerce, riches, and cleanliness, to an extraordinary degree, all those cantons that contain a majority of Catholic inhabitants.

Assertions of this character are more rash than correct, and only impose on those who are unacquainted with the history of Switzerland.

The basin of the Lake of Leman has received from nature the gift of an exceptionally fertile soil, and exceptionally economical resources.

It is no marvel, therefore, that the populations who inhabit these favoured districts should be more prosperous than those of the mountainous villages in Uri, or in the wild valleys of Saas, Anniviers, and Dermatt in the Haut-Valais.

If a comparison be made between the Protestant country districts of Vaud, not in the basin of the Lake of Leman, and the Catholic districts of the canton of Fribourg, which have the same climate and are at the same altitude, it will be seen that the Catholics of Fribourg are in no way inferior to the Protestant inhabitants of Vaud, either as regards intellectual attainments, order, or well-being.

The prosperity of Geneva is natural, and there is no necessity to pay homage to the co-religionists of M. Carteret, for the sake of explaining it. The town occupies an exceptionally good position, close to France, on the borders of a large lake, covered with steamboats, and surrounded by vineyards and rich pasture land, and has been from time immemorial a place of great resort for strangers from all parts of the world.

The prosperity of Neufchatel is due to its population of clock-makers, as much Catholic as Protestant, but whose lot in any case is not very enviable. It is as unreasonable to say that the cantons of Geneva and Neufchatel are more prosperous than those of the Haut-Valais and the forest cantons, because they are Protestant, as it would be to attribute the impossibility of planting corn-fields on the slopes of Mount Cervin, or vines in the fields of Andermatt and Uri, to the Catholicism of the inhabitants.

M. Martin ("*Avenir du Protestantisme et du Catholicisme,*" p. 197) states with reference to the canton of Valais as an "economical" fact, that at a general meeting of the Society of St. Vincent de Paul, at St. Maurice, the conference of the Valais declared they did not know how to employ the funds of the Society, since *they had no poor persons in their district.*

On the strength of Hepworth Dixon's works on Switzerland, the assertion has been made that in the canton of Appenzel (since 1597 divided into the two districts of Inner-Rhoden in the mountains, inhabited by 11,900 Catholics, and Ausser-Rhoden in the valley, inhabited by 46,726 Protestants) the Protestants are active, industrious, sociable, and rich; the Catholics lazy, ignorant, poor, creatures of habit, and dispersed in scattered huts. He writes as follows:—

"Each shepherd lives apart from his fellows, whom he only meets at mass, at wrestling matches, and public-houses.

The lads can read and write, for they are Switzers subject to the cantonal law, but books and journals are unknown amongst them, saving here and there some histories of the lives of the saints and popular papers containing scraps of old wives' lore, in place of general and exciting news."

The "Saturday Review" (No. 853) does not consider Hepworth Dixon a trustworthy authority, so that any line of arguments built upon his statements would probably be considered unsatisfactory in the eyes of a large class of persons.

We quote this fact in order that our readers may rest assured that no prejudice on our part makes us discredit the evidence given in relation to Switzerland. It stands to reason that a widely-scattered population of herdsmen living in mountainous districts, that are almost inaccessible, must be more wild and poverty-stricken than a population dwelling in a valley full of towns and villages. The religious question has nothing in common with the economical condition of the canton of Appenzel.

Hepworth Dixon's picture, stripped of its wrongly-drawn accompaniments, has doubtless many attractions. These mountaineers, renowned throughout the whole of Switzerland for their jovial temperament, their vigour of body and of mind, and their ancient popular games (*Schwingfeste*), must produce a charming effect, when they come down from their dwellings in their picturesque national costumes, either to go to mass or to take some amusement amongst the civilized inhabitants of the valley.

But as long as they are content with reading the lives of the saints and local popular papers, instead of satiating themselves with such literature as is read by the English labouring classes, it is evident they can never expect to have their praises sung either by Hepworth Dixon or any of the school of modern liberals.

CHAPTER III.

COMPARISON BETWEEN CATHOLIC AND PROTESTANT COUNTRIES FROM AN ECONOMICAL POINT OF VIEW.

The true signification of the expression "a man of the day"—First temporal rule of human societies—How a society of uncivilized people may be relatively perfect—Incorrectness of statement that Protestant countries are more active and industrious than Catholic countries—Political economy of the Catholics in Prussia—In the United States of America—In Canada—French Protestantism—Economical consequences of the revocation of the Edict of Nantes—The rate of exchange in Catholic countries—Catholics and the book trade—Political life in Germany.

EFORE further entangling ourselves in the labyrinth of the deductive school, we will once more recall the principles which predominate in this discussion.

We may begin by asserting that we have a profound admiration for all the scientific discoveries of our day ;

and that we appreciate the practical importance of industry and of commerce.

We are "men of the day," but we are nevertheless disposed to think that it would be difficult to prove that Aristotle was a philosopher of lower merit than M. Tiberghien, that Alexander of Macedonia was inferior in political knowledge and experience to Prince Bismarck, that Demosthenes was less clever and enlightened than Mr. Gladstone, that Papinien was a pedant compared to Professor Bluntschli, and that M. de Savornin merits a hundredfold higher position in the social scale than St. Jerome.

Protestant sects, and even the Catholic Church itself, have but indirect relations with the great events that these names recall to our memory.

Jesus Christ has said "My kingdom is not of this world."

"Seek first the kingdom of God and His justice, and all the rest shall be added unto you."

This "rest" Catholics possess, as we have said before, in various degrees, and at least to quite as great an extent as Protestants.

At a time when professors of political economy and other great ones of the world look upon themselves as the high priests of the future, because they expose the laws which control the production and the circulation of passing riches and study the conditions of material prosperity, it is necessary to repeat incessantly and proclaim aloud upon the house-tops, that the end of man upon earth does not entirely consist in the exaltation of his well-being.

We find in the catechism authorized for use in the diocese of Malines, a few simple questions and answers which surpass in beauty the "Timée" of Plato and the twelfth book of Aristotle's "Metaphysics:"—

" What is man ? Man is a creature of God, gifted with reason, possessing an immortal soul and a mortal body. Which is the noblest part of man ? The soul. For what end did God create man ? Man was created by God to serve Him in this life and to possess Him eternally in the next. Are we then not created to enjoy ourselves in this life and to amass riches ? No, we are created to serve God."

To serve God is to reign. *Servire Deo, regnare est.*

He who serves God truly, reigns over creation, even though he may be the poorest and most illiterate of men. The Christian faith was not preached and the Universal Church was not founded either by rich capitalists, literary and scientific writers, professors of rural economy, consummate politicians, clever diplomatists, great generals, or shrewd and eloquent lawyers.

Jesus Christ, *filius fabri*, lived the life of an artisan, and died crucified between two malefactors; the Apostles were simple labourers and fishermen, and the whole work of Christianity was the greatest scandal which "the learned," "the rich," "the intelligent," "the civilized," of the first four centuries were called upon to witness.

It is the same at the present day: the existence, the development, the immutability of the Catholic Church together form a scandal in the eyes of unbelievers, and of those who are entirely given up to the pleasures of the world.

Until now the man of the "tertiary period," who, it was supposed, would be the same triumph in the natural theology of rationalism as the invention of the Krupp cannon has been in military art, has not yet been discovered, but cities built on piles do still exist which to the horror of modern liberals are still in the hands of the clergy.

M. X. Marmier not long ago gave a dissertation before the various assembled Academies of France, on the history of the dwellings of different nations,

From an Economical Point of View.

from which we select an interesting passage relating to the cities that are built upon piles :—

"In one of the most fertile regions of South America, in the Republic of Venezuela, a tribe of Indians may be found who have constructed their dwellings in the middle of the lake of Maracaibo, not in order to escape from tigers or serpents, or the invasion of hostile tribes, but to withdraw themselves from a legion of mosquitoes, far larger and more venomous than those that frequent our European climate. These insects, as is well-known in all countries, prefer the neighbourhood of water, but scarcely ever leave the damp soil on the bank where they were hatched, and the Indians know that a certain distance from the shore they are safe from their attacks. They are surrounded with everything necessary to build huts, the *palo di hierro*, for their piles, a lighter sort of wood for their floors and partitions, creeping plants out of which they can make ropes for binding together the different parts of the building, and palm leaves as a covering for the roof.

There is no need to build massive walls (rain being the only kind of inclement weather they have to dread), for snow, frost, and cold winds are unknown. Thanks to the great riches of the country, there is no trouble as to the means of existence.

The lake is full of fish, and at certain seasons of the year thousands of wild ducks come and settle, of which large numbers are captured by means of snares.

The *nevea*, from which a milky sap is extracted that forms india-rubber, grows plentifully along the banks, and traders come every year to buy this article, as well as the down of the ducks, and the cargoes of smoked and preserved fish which this industrious people collect. These Indians live in their peaceful settlement, and are not ranked amongst civilized nations ; they possess no newspapers and have no railways ; they are ignorant of the sweet excitements connected with the rise and fall of the Funds, and of the charm of parliamentary discussions.

But they are Christians (converted by Spanish missionaries), and in the midst of their simple village rises a church built on piles.

The cross that crowns the summit of the steeple is reflected in the shining mirror of water, and the bell peals forth the angelus in this solitude of the New World; at the hours of service, the family canoes are grouped around its entrance, whilst the faithful Indians devoutly kneel within its precincts.

When the Spaniards first arrived in this quarter the sight of the aquatic dwellings of Maracaibo reminded them of Venice, and they christened the country they had discovered by the name of Venezuela.

The opulent and proud Venice of the old world has now lost her riches; the city of the Doges has lost her golden ring, the Queen of the Adriatic has forfeited her crown, and she who was at one time so full of glory has been subjected to numberless disasters; but this little Indian tribe of Venezuela has never known such splendid prosperity, and will never experience such a terrible downfall.

Contented with its humble position in the world, it neither dreams of growing rich by rash speculation, nor increasing its boundaries by adventurous conquest.

The lake on which it is situated is its vast ocean, its frail bark is its '*Bucentoro,*' its wooden chapel is its basilica of St. Mark, and its prosperity consists in the modest and simple habits of its daily life."

It is not probable that either we or our readers would select this city on piles as a summer residence; but we should never presume to assert that these contented and happy people live, before God, in a state of civilization inferior to that enjoyed by the officials of the existing government at Geneva, or the police agents of Berlin.

The inference we wish to draw from this kind of simile is that the deductive theories of the school of modern continental liberals are in their origin and essence fallacious. The material and exterior development of a society depends upon nature, and a variety of accessory circumstances which differ according to times and places.

The only one thing that is necessary, everywhere, and at all times, is the service of God; and even if a people, in the accomplishment of this service, should fail in politics, economy, industry, or literature, they would nevertheless remain superior to all the things of this world. *Servire Deo, regnare est.*

We do not deny the possibility of any Catholic society (even if religiously perfect) under the influence of certain exterior circumstances showing symptoms of temporary decline; but we entirely repudiate the assertion that "wherever the two forms of worship co-exist in a country, the Protestants are more active, more industrious, more economical, and consequently richer than the Catholics."

Considering that the end of life is not only the

amassing of riches, we might content ourselves with quoting the well-known words of Melancthon to his mother, "Though it may be better to live as a Protestant, it is preferable to die a Catholic;" but our assertion is that a reasonably economical development does not smother the spiritual means that man must employ in order to arrive at his supernatural end.

In Prussia (the stronghold of Lutheranism) the Catholic provinces of the Rhine, Westphalia, and Silesia are the richest and most prosperous portions of the whole kingdom, whilst the Protestant districts of Pomerania and Brandenbourg are the poorest and most destitute, besides producing the largest number of emigrants.

In the actual district of Prussia proper, the Catholic portion of Ermeland is vastly superior in wealth and civilization to the remainder, which is Protestant.

Posen is certainly less prosperous than the other Catholic provinces, though possessing a robust and sturdy class of peasants; but the reason for this may be traced to the errors of the governments of the old Polish monarchy, and to the fact that it suffers at present from an administrative tyranny that stifles every aspiration.

The government at Berlin has sworn to Germanize

the whole duchy of Posen; and to accomplish this end all the teaching in the elementary schools is given in the German language, even to children who have learnt from their parents nothing but Polish.

The intellectual growth of the young is stunted with determinate and fixed purpose, and the economical development of the whole people is dwarfed by the action of the government in the elementary schools.

Frederic II., subsequently to the annexation of the Catholic district of Westphalia to the electorate of Brandenbourg, gave permission to the inhabitants of the former to settle in the territory of the latter, with the exception of the town of Berlin, which was absolutely prohibited to them.

This is the secret of the large number of Catholic families to be found in the present day throughout the Margravate (Westphalians in their origin).

Most of these families live in easy, if not affluent, circumstances, in the midst of a relatively poor district. Since the proclamation of religious liberty in the year 1850, they have served as the nursery of all the Catholic missions in that part of the country.

Many poor localities may be found in Silesia and Posen, but they are almost invariably the spots where large monasteries had existed previous to their secularization in 1810 and 1831.

The people that dwelt around these old institutions, and who partook in their prosperity and splendour, found themselves suddenly ruined the moment the source of long-established prosperity was dried up, the ancient causes of their industry swept away, and their benefactors suppressed.

Such desolation (the result of a Protestant spirit of animosity) naturally takes a long period for recovery.

The fact is, that in mixed countries, where the majority does not exercise any violent oppression, the minority by the concentration of its strength and its energy is generally distinguished by an industrious activity.

Such is the cause of the industry and commerce of the Greeks in the Turkish Empire, of the Protestants in Bavaria, Alsace, and the south of France, of the Catholics in Holland, of the Dalmatians in the old republic of Venice, of the Chinese in the English possessions in Asia, and of the Jews in every quarter of the globe.

Look at the Catholics throughout the New World; who can deny the vast progress they have made?

M. de Tocqueville, a well-known writer, makes the following remarkable statements in a work on democracy:[1]—

"America is the most democratic country in the world, and is at the same time that in which the Catholic religion makes the greatest progress.

Future generations will tend more and more to the formation of two opposite parties, the one altogether setting aside the teaching of Christianity, the other retiring into the fold of the Catholic Church."

And again :—

"The American Protestant preachers dwell much upon earthly considerations in their discourses, and appear to me to have great difficulty in speaking of anything else.

In order to please their congregations and accommodate their hearers, they attempt to prove how greatly religious opinions favour civil liberty and public order. It is difficult to realize from their discourses whether the principal object of religion is to attain eternal happiness in the next world, or to enjoy comfort and well-being in the present." (*Idem*, p. 32.)

The first Catholic bishop appointed in the United States was Monsignor Carroll, in the year 1790. At the present time (1876) there are seven archbishops and thirty-six bishops, and quite recently an American prelate has for the first time been admitted into the sacred College of Cardinals.

---

[1] *See* "Democracy in America." By M. de Tocqueville. Vol. ii. page 30, 3rd edition. Paquerre, Paris, 1850.

(Monsignor MacCloskey, Archbishop of New York, was raised to this dignity in the early part of the year 1875, by his Holiness Pope Pius IX.)

Catholic works of every kind are on the increase, and the faithful of Louisiana, Missouri, the Western States, California, and Oregon, are well able to compete with the ancient and wealthy Catholic communities of New England.

These innumerable works are endowed with a capital, the palpable manifestation of an unexampled prosperity.

We do not know much respecting the wealth of the Canadian Catholics, but we have never heard of their poverty.

In the island of Newfoundland, and in Lower Canada, where the descendants of the original French colonists form two-thirds of the population, the greater portion of the landed property of the country is in the hands of the Catholics, who in most cases live in easy and affluent circumstances. In Upper Canada the Catholics, few in number, are principally immigrants from Ireland and Germany, and are in the same condition as all that class of colonists throughout the British possessions.

From the time of the annexation of the French

colonies of North America to the English Crown, the Catholics have been, if not actually oppressed, certainly deprived of the favours of the mother country, and it is a remarkable fact, and one worthy of the attention of our opponents, that they are the only people who since the end of the last century have remained faithful to the English Crown, a fidelity which has been rewarded by a very tardy display of gratitude on the part of England.

During the last forty years, however, the Canadian Catholics have been free to make their own efforts, and in this short space of time have manifested a prodigious amount of activity.

The enterprising and practical spirit of the English people, which existed long before the birth of Protestantism, has shown itself in Canada, as elsewhere, and we freely admit that in industrial and commercial speculations "perfidious Albion" truly occupies the first place in the world; but we repeat what we have more than once stated, that prosperity and wealth are not the standard of the moral and political value either of the individual, the family, the society, or the nation.

On the faith of the Canadian people themselves, English Protestants do not occupy the first places either at Quebec, Montreal, or even at St. John's, Newfoundland.

Quebec in Canada and Nismes in the south of France are places widely apart from each other, but both contain a population of French people, the former afflicted with Catholicism, the latter transformed by the Reformation: it is to this latter place, the birthplace of the great Guizot, that we wish to make some allusion.

M. Audiganne, in a remarkable work upon the "Working Population of France," notices the superiority of the Protestant party, in the matter of industry, which work is the less open to suspicion since he does not attribute this superiority to Protestantism.

The majority of the working classes at Nismes, he declares, are Catholic, especially amongst the silk-weavers, whilst the heads of the financial and commercial establishments and all the capitalists belong, as a rule, to the reformed religion.

When one family is divided into two branches, the one having remained faithful to the Church of its ancestors, the other having embraced the new doctrines, there is in almost every case a progressive poverty on the one side, and an increase of wealth on the other.

At Mazamet, the Elbœuf of the south of France, according to the same writer, the heads of all the large firms are Protestants, whilst the great majority of the operatives are Catholics. He also asserts that there is less instruction amongst the latter than amongst the labouring families of the Protestants.

Economical facts like these are easy to account for, and M. Audiganne is careful to say that he does not attribute to religious causes a state of things which at first sight appears so favourable to the Protestant side.

Not so M. de Laveleye, who coolly divides this testimony, to suit his theories; and whilst ignoring all that is unfavourable, he takes for his argument only that portion which supports his own opinion.

Even granting that this method of procedure in discussion is admissible in the domain of modern logic, what conclusion can be drawn?

At the most, a fact interesting to note down, that at Nismes and Mazamet nearly all the funded wealth is in the hands of the Protestants.

Otherwise, the Messrs. Rothschild, as the richest people in Europe, must be considered as possessed of a civilization superior to that of the Protestants in the Old or New World; the Jewish bankers of Frankfort and Berlin, to the followers of Luther in Germany ; and the Jews, as a body, vastly superior to the whole race of Protestants.

In the face of the present scandalous abuse and destruction of religious liberty in Switzerland and Germany, it was scarcely necessary to allude to past abuses such as the revocation of the Edict of Nantes, as M. de Laveleye does in the following terms :—

> "Before the revocation of the Edict of Nantes, the reformers excelled in every branch of industry, and the Catholics, who could not cope with them, prohibited them in the year 1662 by several successive edicts from the exercise of various branches of trade in which they had attained great perfection.
>
> After their expulsion from France, the Protestants carried with them into England, Prussia, and Holland their spirit of enterprise, industry, and economy, and enriched the districts in which they settled.
>
> It is to people of the Latin race, who had embraced the reformed religion, that the Teutons owe in part their progress.
>
> The refugees of the revocation of the Edict of Nantes introduced into England many kinds of industry, amongst others the silk trade, and the civilization of the Scotch may be regarded as the work of the disciples of Calvin."

Calvinist civilization in Scotland !

In the whole history of Christianity there is not a sect to be found whose action has been more rough, more intolerant, and more brutal.

We have already lifted a corner of the veil that some

persons wish to throw over the condition of Scotland in bygone days, and at another time we shall have occasion to lift it still higher.

For the present we will consider the question of the revocation of the Edict of Nantes.

This impolitic act of Louis XIV., according to the testimony of Macaulay and Ranke, was neither approved of by the Cabinet of Madrid nor by Pope Innocent XI., as a careful study of their writings can testify.

When Englishmen inveigh against Louis XIV.'s unfortunate revocation of that act, they seem to forget that at that very time the laws of England were inflicting the penalty of death on any Catholic priest who ventured to offer the sacrifice of the Mass within this realm.

Quite independently of any alleged cruelties on the part of Catholic nations, Scotch and Genevan Calvinists, German Lutherans, and the tyrannical disciples of Henry VIII., Elizabeth, Barlow and Parker, have no right to reproach Louis XIV. for any act of intolerance, when the history of each of these people is stained by so much cruelty and tyranny.

Louis XIV. used severity towards the French reformers quite as much, if not more, from political than from religious reasons, whilst the Protestant party throughout Europe have invariably acted, and in some places still continue to act with severity against Catholics, from mere hatred of Catholicism and detestation of the fundamental principles of the Church. Germany and Switzerland at the present day afford a striking example of our assertion.

Is there a single Catholic country in the world that treats its Protestant subjects in the cavalier fashion that Prussia and Switzerland have thought fit to adopt towards the Catholics?

The king of France called the theological "thesis" to his aid, and in overturning the "hypothesis" of the religious liberty of the dissidents, did not boast of the principles of the Reformation as regarded liberty of worship.

As to the economical side of the question of the expulsion of the Huguenots, many considerations might be entered into, but we will content ourselves with contesting the facts quoted by a reference to an article in the "*Revue des Questions Historiques*" (vol. xv. p. 590, in 1874), upon a work of M. de Segur Dupeyron, formerly French consul at Antwerp, entitled, "History of the Maritime and Commercial Negotiations of France in the Seventeenth and

Eighteenth Centuries, considered in their relation to General Politics."

M. de Segur Dupeyron blames the act of Louis XIV., and attributes the momentary decline of French industry, during the second half of his reign, to the misfortunes of war, and denies that the prosperity of other countries has been the work of French refugees.

The cloth trade of Friesland dates from the Carlovingian period; and at the beginning of the sixteenth century Amsterdam and Leyden manufactured 24,000 pieces of cloth every year.

The weaving of wool was introduced into England by Flemish artisans two centuries before the preaching of Luther.

Seventy years before the revocation of the Edict of Nantes a few workmen of Aix-la-Chapelle started a new method for the manufacture of woollen goods in the town of Amsterdam, and five-and-twenty years previous to this silk manufactories had been already organized in Holland.

The present perfected methods of weaving woollen materials were introduced into Sedan and the south of France by Dutch and Flemish workmen.

The silk trade was first introduced into France about the year 1521 by artisans from the plains of

Lombardy. From the year 1629 to 1681 it was organized in London, and 4,000 workmen were employed; and in the year 1713 (that is to say, twenty-eight years after the revocation of the Edict of Nantes) the number of operatives remained the same.

A diplomatic letter of 1686 makes known the fact that the industry of linen, flax, and hemp was brought to perfection in Great Britain by French *Catholic* artizans.

In the year 1713 the English manufactories were incapable of keeping up competition with the French, and this fact is made evident by the petitions to the English Parliament against the project of a treaty that was being negotiated at Utrecht.

The case is precisely similar as regards Holland.

The author of the "History of the Protestant Refugees" tells us that the industry of the refugees was less durable in Holland than its brilliant beginning had given hopes of.

The manufactories of silk, of linen, and of paper, which they had called into existence, began to decline as early as the first half of the eighteenth century, *i.e.* after the re-establishment of peace.

The same author adds that the woollen and leather trade, and the refineries of sugar, preserve to this day the improvements which date from that period—a theory which M. de Segur Dupeyron denies in showing that all the existing improvements of these trades are very much posterior to the year 1685.

The conclusion of the "History of the Protestant Refugees" is that the manufactories established by the French exiles could not fail to dwindle away by degrees.

The fabrication of silk only flourished till the close of the war of the Spanish Succession (1713).

On the restoration of peace the French silks, which were less costly and at the same time combined better work with greater elegance and taste, soon regained their old superiority over the Dutch markets.

M. de Segur Dupeyron concludes in the following words:—

"In the presence of French competition it was almost impossible for the Protestant refugees to establish anything durable either in England or in Holland."

In Prussia, where enormous advantages were offered to the refugees, the industry of which they encouraged the development was only able to be sustained by a series of exceptional laws and prohibitions. We must attribute the origin of this design to a determination on the part of the elector of Brandenbourg to escape in his possessions, by means of the protectionist system, the industrial monopoly of Holland and Great Britain.

He offered such exorbitant conditions that he was enabled to import into his territory workmen from every other.

The ancestors of Ancillon, Dubois, Reymond, De l'Estocq, De Forcade, Clairon d'Haussonville, Brassier de St. Simon, Chapuis, Fournier, &c., and, in fact, most of the ancestors of the Protestant party in France, sought for position in the ranks of the army, the clergy, and the civil administration rather than in trade or commerce.

The silk manufactories suffered in France during the war of the Spanish Succession, but once peace was concluded, neither England nor Holland was able to compete with a revival of French industry.

The English and Dutch manufactories showed a marvellous development during the same war, but after the proclamation of peace their industry returned to its former condition.

We consider these indications amply sufficient to reduce to their proper worth assertions respecting the economical consequences of the revocation of the Edict of Nantes.

From an Economical Point of View. 91

We next pass to the question of the funds. M. de Laveleye says—

"If we compare the quotations on the exchange of the public funds of Protestant and Catholic States, we shall find a great difference. The English 3 per cents are above 92; the French 3 per cents average 60; the Dutch, Prussian, Danish, and Swedish funds are at least at par; in Austria, Italy, Spain, and Portugal they are lower by 30 or 50 per cent."

It is ungenerous of him to include Italy in this catalogue, since that kingdom in its modern aspect is the work of the continental liberals, but we will examine how much truth there is in his assertions.

Before the year 1859 the finances of the States of the Church, the kingdom of Naples, the duchies of Modena, Parma, and Tuscany, and above all of the kingdom of Piedmont and Venetian Lombardy, were in a most prosperous condition.

Before the general revolution throughout Europe in 1848, which it may be as well to remind our readers was the work of the liberal party, Austrian currency was above par.

Dutch finance is no more due to Protestantism than Belgian finance is due to Catholicism.

No one would dispute the unparalleled splendour of English wealth, but it should be borne in mind that

Tyre also was rich, Spain was wealthy, and Babylon powerful, but their riches have passed away. The ancient princes of Mexico possessed riches which the conquering Spaniards would scarcely credit, and if Tiberius had issued a loan, it would have been covered a thousand times over.

The grandfather of the present M. de Rothschild was a man of humble birth and means, and his great-grandchildren may be reduced to mediocrity, but these circumstances prove nothing, either for or against Judaism.

If after another war the Lutheran Prussians have to collect ten thousand millions, as the Catholic French found themselves compelled to do in 1871, we shall see whether the call will meet with equal response, and whether the sum will be five times the amount demanded.

Another argument that has been advanced to prove the superiority of Protestantism is that in Germany the trade in intellectual works, such as books, reviews, maps, and newspapers, is almost entirely in the hands of Jews and Protestants; but surely if Protestants only occupy the second place in this medley of non-Catholic civilization, it is to Judaism and not Protestantism that our modern liberals should turn their attention.

From an Economical Point of View.

The commerce of works of the mind in Germany is a subject that requires more than mere incidental treatment. The book trade, for example, is centred in Leipzig, with so great a power that the market of Berlin has itself in vain attempted to compete with it. This centre of the book trade is so strongly influenced by Protestant and Jewish ideas, that Catholic publications are practically excluded.

Since the year 1848 Catholic publishers have been obliged to resort to extraordinary and special methods in order to obtain a circulation for the works they bring out; for it must not be forgotten that previous to that year there was no *liberty* in the country of Luther for productions of the mind.

The absolute proceedings on the part of the Leipzig book market are one of the secondary causes of the philosophical and literary decline of the Germany of to-day and of the materialism into which the book-trade is perpetually falling.

It is not only Catholic works that are excluded from the central depôt, any works not favourably disposed towards the *national liberal party* remain unnoticed. This fact may be exemplified by the case of Herr Wuttke, a staunch Protestant of the old school, and a distinguished professor in the University of Leipzig.

One of his works, entitled "The Press and the Formation of Public Opinion in Germany," has been entirely ignored, not only in the enlightened districts of North Germany, but even in Leipzig itself.

It is satisfactory to note that in spite of this studied contempt on the part of the Leipzig publishers, the book has gone through three editions.

The special library reviews of German publications, that are so loquacious and often so ridiculously prolific, either take no notice of Catholic publications or print them in small type, in an obscure part of the catalogue. Partiality of this character called forth the creation of new library reviews especially intended for Catholic publications.

Amongst these may be mentioned the "*Litterarischer Handweisser*," established about thirteen years ago in Westphalia by Dr. Hulskamp and the late Dr. H. Rump.

This monthly review, preceded by biographical and other notices, and written in a style peculiarly suitable and elegant, is a perfect model for persons of literary and scientific tastes. It forms a kind of encyclopædia, having an index which contains notices of contemporary publications in England, America, France, and Germany. There does not exist, so far as we know, in contemporary literature, with the exception of the "*Poly-biblion,*" and the French "*Bibliographie Catholique,*" a collection superior to it.

Since the year 1848 Catholic libraries have spread themselves over Germany, several of which have in that short space of time acquired European celebrity, and in this way the exclusiveness of the Leipzig book market has proved beneficial to Catholic publications.

There is now no town of any size or importance, either in the purely Catholic or semi-Catholic districts, that does not possess one or more Catholic publishers.

The intolerance of Protestant and Jewish merchants has been rivalled by the compilers of the celebrated encyclopædias. One of the latest and most extraordinary instances of this unseemly partiality on the part of men of science, is that recently exhibited by the son-in-law of Schelling, M. G. Waitz, in his encyclopædia of German historical science.

The studied and obstinate refusal of justice on the part of the most renowned authors of the dominant school has been recently stigmatized in a brilliant article in the review of Mayence ("*Der Catholik,*" October, 1875).

Since the appearance of Herr Wuttke's work,[1] a certain amount of presumption is necessary to sing the praises of the German anti-Catholic press, a press almost exclusively in the hands of the Jews in a country destined to be for ever notorious on account of its *reptile fund*.[2]

The Catholic daily press is in no way inferior to the free-thinking papers, either in literary merit or power.

In the whole German empire there is no newspaper superior in composition and style to the courageous and energetic organ of the Catholics of Berlin, called the "*Germania*," a paper which has become a power, at the very doors of the chancellor of the empire. Prince Bismarck himself, in the spring of 1874, being attacked by the editor, Abbé Majunke, who was also a deputy of the Reichstag, for having prohibited it in Alsace, admitted its power and ability, whilst he designated certain editors of the official journals as *swineherds* ("*sauhirten*").

---

[1] The English and German press have been completely silent on the subject of this interesting work, which has passed through three editions.

[2] *Reptile fund.* This refers to the money paid by the government to the various papers in order that they should sing their praises, a great part of the money being that which was taken from the King of Hanover.

The "*Kölnischer Volkszeitung*," published by Herr Bachem, at Cologne, is one of the best written and most energetic of European newspapers.

No town of any importance in the Catholic or semi-Catholic districts, since the year 1848 (the time that the liberty of the press has been tolerated in Germany), has been without a Catholic periodical of some sort.

The greater portion of the German press, with the honourable exceptions of the "*Neue Preussischer Zeitung*," the "*Frankfurter Zeitung*," and one or two others, are the creatures of the government, and largely subsidized by its funds; but the Catholic papers (about three hundred in number), maintain a noble attitude of self-respect and independence.

Without subsidies, without any *reptile fund*, without the support of the "business world," they increase and prosper, though harassed by perpetual prosecutions and suspensions.

The "*Germania*" has had the honour, in the short space of three years, of having had five of its editorial staff and contributors condemned to imprisonment. The powers of the government, the influence of the police, and the zeal of the courts of justice are directed against the expansion of the Catholic press, which displays a marvellous amount of life and vigour. The amendments which the Prussian government lately proposed to introduce into the penal code would seem to have been suggested for no other purpose than to exterminate it, and to verify once more those celebrated words of Joseph de Maistre, "*Error, unless supported by proscription, can never hold its own against truth.*"

In the whole of Germany there is no periodical that exercises more influence on general public opinion than the "Historical and Political Review" of Munich (the "Yellow Book," as it is called), ably conducted by Messrs. Joerg and Binder, and founded by Joseph Görres, the great Catholic writer, whom Napoleon I. christened "*the sixth power.*"

Since the death of this celebrated man, and the deaths of Schlegel, Eichendorf, and the Austrian Grilsparger (who were all Catholics), and Heine (a Jew), Germany has produced no great writer.

The literature of that country is now divided between a certain materialistic originality, and an imitation of the faults of the existing literature of France, a mediocrity which finds favour.

The language of Schiller, which Prince Bismarck so arrogantly attempted to introduce into German diplomatic transactions with foreign countries, makes no progress.

The affected use of new terms, incomprehensible to the uninitiated, and of words borrowed from the English and French, would prevent it from ever becoming generally practicable.

When the Prussian government recently addressed the Belgian cabinet in this fashion, it took three persons a whole evening—two of whom were Germans—to determine the sense of certain phrases, just as if it had been a Persian satire, or an Assyrian inscription that had to be deciphered.

The German parliament, with the exception of Herr Lasker (a Jew) and Prince Bismarck, contains but few orators on the liberal side of the house, whereas amongst the centre, or Catholic party, we find a whole band of debaters—Windhorst (the pearl of Meppen), Peter and August Reichensperger, the Baron de Schorlemer-Alst (captain of the Westphalian peasants), Canon Moufang, and Dr. Joerg.

An investigation amongst the lower classes proves that amongst the Catholics alone is there any real political life.

The entire population breathes and lives in its clergy and its deputies.

They alone display the political maturity which gives energy in the defence of right, calmness in passive resistance against injustice, perseverance in dignified protests; and they alone amongst all the various political sections, make a loyal use of the parliamentary system from which their adversaries have gathered nothing but instruments of despotism and oppression. By a scandalous abuse of the rights of parliamentary majorities, these latter have brought discredit upon representative institutions, preserved intact in most Catholic districts, but neglected or forgotten from the sixteenth century in the margravate of Brandenbourg.

The centre-party at Berlin is supported by as large a number of electors as its liberal adversaries, though the latter have a majority in parliament three times as numerous. It has been ascertained as a fact that 99 per cent. of the Catholic electors record their votes, whereas the liberals scarcely obtain 50 per cent. in their electoral colleges.

The German liberals recently stigmatized the Catholics as an "electoral herd of cattle" ("*stimmvieh*"), but the term is rather beside the mark in the mouths of men who were publicly informed by their chief, Prince Bismarck, that they were *elected in his name to do his bidding*.

The truth of the statement is evident, and it is universally admitted that the chancellor of the German empire contains within his person alone (the Catholic party, of course, excepted) the whole political life of Germany. We should have considered the term "electoral herd of cattle" was more appropriate as the designation of the national liberal party.

It is unnecessary on this point to say more than to refer our readers to the avowals made by Bismarck and his faithful colleague, Dr. Falck, on presenting the project of the Falck laws. They both openly admitted their inability to oppose and contend with the Catholics as long as the Church was allowed freedom, and they therefore counselled the use of force.

At the present moment—thanks to the temporary union of the governing authorities and the national liberal party (who are nominally Protestant)—the entire body of Catholics are hunted like wild beasts, whilst favours and compliments of every kind are showered upon the lukewarm followers of Luther.

The Catholic Church, however, has not been vanquished, nor have her faithful members been overcome—a fact that the liberals themselves unwillingly admit, after only a few years of experience. They have begun to discover, when too late, that Catholics are neither what they have stated them to be, nor what they would wish them to be.

M. Thiers is credited with a saying which contains a great deal of truth, "*Ceux qui mangent du prêtre catholique en meurent.*"

We are assured, again, that the Reformation has communicated to the countries that adopted it a strength that history can scarcely account for.

Sweden, England, Prussia, the Netherlands, and the United States are contrasted with Spain, France, and Austria.

Prussia, in the eyes of M. de Laveleye, is considered worthy of the highest praise, from the fact that it has defeated two empires, each of them much larger than itself—the first in seven weeks, the second in seven months.

An argument of this kind is really astonishing in the mouth of an economist.

At the beginning of the present century Prussia was beaten in a single day at the battle of Jena, but no one would dream of attributing that to Luther or to Protestantism.

This whole series of arguments is illusory. If Spain, France, and Austria have, at certain different epochs, occupied the first place in what is called the concert of nations, it is clear to demonstration that the Catholic religion does not form an obstacle to the temporal greatness of a nation.

If, on the other hand, Holland and Sweden, in bygone days, occupied a preponderating position in the political world, it is evident that Protestantism is not a guarantee against decline.

M. de Laveleye proceeds to prophesy that in two centuries Asia will be in the hands of the schismatic Sclaves, in which case the Greek Church must be superior to Protestantism.

Two centuries ago he admits that the supremacy of Europe belonged incontestably to Catholic States, but, at the present moment, with France, Austria, Spain, Italy, and South America on one side, and Russia, the German empire, England, and the United States of North America on the other, evidently the preponderance has passed to heretics and schismatics.

Italy, formerly but a geographical expression, has only existed as a kingdom since 1859. Up to the year 1865 Austria was not considered inferior to Prussia, and France has only been disregarded since the Franco-German war of 1870. The German empire is but of yesterday, and does not appear to possess the fundamental and essential conditions of durability;

Russia,[1] smarting from defeat ever since the Crimean war, has remained hitherto a passive spectator of European events; and has at length found herself, without any effort on her part, the umpire of Europe.

In a perfectly balanced scale, two grains of powder and shot, whether they be fabricated by Protestants, Catholics, or Greeks, must always be more effective than one grain.

In other words, Russia is at this moment the arbiter of the European equilibrium; Austria may possibly occupy this position to-morrow, and Italy or Spain the day after.

Attempts to depreciate the Catholic Church by means of an economical formula are not by any means new. Napoleon Roussel, a French Protestant clergyman, twenty years ago wrote a work, entitled "Catholic and Protestant Nations, considered under the three-fold aspect of Well-Being, Enlightenment, and Morality."

The work itself was soon forgotten; but a critique on it, written by a clever sceptic, M. John Lemoine, a

---

[1] Since the above was written Russia has defeated Turkey, and, in defiance of all her previous promises, seeks to increase her territory and to dictate to Europe.

member of the French Academy, has lost none of its freshness.

We reproduce it almost *in extenso*, from an excellent pamphlet by Monsignor de Segur, entitled "Remarks on the Protestantism of the Present Day:"—

"We opened this book anxious to say all the good we could of it, but with all the good-will in the world it is impossible to think well of it, or even of the feeling that inspired it. It sets forth the most senseless and despairing materialism, and if a minister of the gospel has no better moral to present to the world, nothing remains for mankind at large than to feed well and be prosperous; the richest man will always be the most virtuous.

In the comparison of Catholic and Protestant nations under the three-fold aspects of well-being, enlightenment, and morality, morality, which ought to occupy the first place, is mentioned last, enlightenment comes second, but well-being and prosperity are given the first rank and brought prominently forward.

In the course of two volumes M. Roussel asserts that Protestants are infinitely happier in this world than Catholics, that they possess larger fortunes, more wealth, and in short greater luxuries of every sort.

Hitherto we had always believed that at the final day of judgment God would place on one side the good, on the other the bad; but according to this theory mankind should be divided into the two categories of rich and poor.

In Protestant theology it would seem that in order to be saved, respectability and wealth are essential.

M. Roussel, as usual with men of his school, contrasts what he is pleased to call the wretchedness of Catholic Ireland with the prosperity of Protestant Scotland, of course to the disparagement of the former, forgetful of the different treatment these countries have received at the hands of the English governments. Like persons suffering from jaundice, who see everything through a yellow glass, he ferrets out the Catholic religion from places where one would scarcely have supposed it would penetrate, and contrasts it with a prosperous and wealthy Scotch county town.

He draws two pictures, one of an Irish fight and the use of the shillelaghs, which he condemns, and another of an English pugilistic encounter, which he deems worthy of all praise.

He enlarges on the qualities of these noble prize-fighters who profess Protestantism, and the admirable blows of the fist which are doubtless inspired by faith.

It is unnecessary to follow M. Roussel in the similar chain of argument applied to Switzerland and other countries; but as regards Ireland, no one would dispute the worldly advantages of the Protestants, nor would anyone who had studied history refuse to allow that the poverty of the Catholics was in a great measure the result of Protestant legislation.

If the Protestant party, for example, represent one-tenth only of the population, by what right did they confiscate the whole of the property and revenues of the Church? And when M. Roussel, in order to prove that the Catholics are no longer oppressed, informs us that they possess a hierarchy composed of four archbishops and twenty-four bishops, and 2,500 churches and over 2,000 priests, ought he not himself to be inspired with some amount of admiration for this poverty-stricken race, who out of their wretchedness and squalor, could yet find the means to support their Church, whilst the Protestant bishops and clergy were in possession of those revenues that anciently belonged to them?

How is it that a man calling himself *a minister of the Gospel* does not bear in mind a certain text, 'Verily, verily, I say unto you, this poor widow has given more than all who have put into the treasury, for they all have given of their abundance; but she of her want has given all she had, even all her substance.' How is it that he can disregard the words of our Lord, ' I say unto you again, it is easier for a camel to go through the eye of a needle than for a rich man to enter into the kingdom of heaven.'"

It is in this way that sectarian spirit blinds many otherwise excellent persons; and in the attempt to put forth moral and religious sentiments, their conclusions become unwittingly in their essence materialistic and anti-Christian. True national prosperity consists in a nation's living so that it may have the majority of its members in a fit state for their entry into another world; and no one can prove that Protestantism is better calculated than Catholicism to produce such a result.

CHAPTER IV.

CATHOLICS AND COLONIZATION.

The pretended sterility of Catholic nations—Meaning of the word colonization—Catholics in the Philippine Islands—In India—English colonies—Dutch colonies—Catholicism in the United States—Colonization of missionaries.

OMAN Catholic nations seem stricken with sterility, they no longer colonize, and they seem to possess no powers of expansion.

The expression, *viduitas et sterilitas*, made use of by M. Thiers to describe the city of Rome, might equally well be applied to them.

Their past has no doubt been brilliant, but the present is gloomy, and their future prospect calculated to cause uneasiness.

Such is the language used by our opponents.

No man of impartiality could accept such statements.

Catholics and Colonization. 109

Never at any epoch of the world's history has Rome been less inactive and less like a widow, never has she given less symptoms of sterility.

Never has the world witnessed the display of greater extremes of devotion and hostility towards the See of Peter, *capitoli immobile saxum*, than at the present.

Does anyone imagine that it is merely for the sake of admiring the ruins of the town of the Cæsars, or studying the recent projects of Garibaldi, that such masses of pilgrims flock thither from all quarters of the globe ? Setting aside the triple crown of the tiara, we ask in all seriousness, is there in the whole universe a single individual who bears so unmistakably stamped on his forehead the sign of royalty, as the present pontiff, Pius IX. ?[1]

Has there been in the last six centuries any Pope whose teachings, injunctions, and even simple recommendations have been more productive of result ?

The re-establishment of a territorial hierarchy in Holland and England, the organization of more than fifty dioceses in America, the foundation of the vast

---

[1] Since the above was written Pope Pius IX. has died, and the accents of praise in which he has been spoken of by the Protestant and Liberal press throughout Europe testify to the truth of our remark. The reflection will apply equally to the present Pontiff, Leo XIII.

churches of the United States, of Australia, Tasmania, &c. &c., and the colossal undertakings accomplished by the College of the Propaganda, have slight appearance of sterility.[1]

At no period of her history has the Church, the Spouse of Christ, been more closely united to her earthly head, and shown greater symptoms of life and vigour, than at present.

Witness the proclamation of the Dogma of the Immaculate Conception, the Œcumenical Council of 1871, the constitution *Dei filius*, the principal works of philosophy upon the relations between reason and faith, the constitution *Pastor æternus*, the encyclicals, *Mirari vos* and *Quanta cura*, put forward as a warning against the debased tendencies of modern continental liberalism, and a score of other important documents addressed *urbi et orbi*.

At what epoch have schisms and heresies been less dangerous for the unity of the Universal Church?[2]

---

[1] The last act of Pius IX. was the decree for the re-establishment of the hierarchy in Scotland.

[2] Alt-Catholicism, a sect commenced under the most favourable circumstances and nurtured in the bosom of the strongest military power on the Continent, has disappointed even the most sanguine. A proof of this is supplied by an official organ of German Protestantism, entitled "*Evangelische Lutherische*

The personal devotion shown to the Pope himself, as governor of the Universal Church, is one of the most remarkable characteristics of the present century.

We can understand from a certain point of view that a sincere opponent of the papacy may be alarmed at facts like these, but we are at a loss to see how anyone can deny them unless he is totally blind.

The nations that are subject to Rome no longer colonize! Who then do colonize?

To whose credit must we place all the colonies at present existing in the world if not to Catholics? The Church is the only institution that has known and still knows how to colonize, according to the testimony of all history.

To colonize a country, according to the historical sense of the word, is to extend to it the benefits of civilization.

For this reason therefore the pirates, or manufactur-

Kirchenzeitung" (1878), which says that from the first it never believed in its vitality or power. The article concludes thus:—
" At first they (the Alt-Catholics) thought of abiding by the decisions of the Council of Trent, but before long they were compelled to enter upon an alliance with the Greek, the Jansenist, the American Dissenting Churches, as well as with the Anglican and German æsthetic Protestants. It cannot be said that Alt-Catholicism has done anything worthy of notice."

ing Anglo-Saxons, who in the last and present centuries have colonized territories by means of eradicating the native population at the very outset, cannot, strictly speaking, be called colonists.

The English and Dutch are doubtless worthy of great respect, but we should never look to their colonial policy for fresh cause for admiration.

The most beautiful colonies of modern times (until the era of the French Revolution of 1789) are due to Spain, Portugal, and France during a period when they were more thoroughly subject to Rome than they are at the present time. The period when these colonies began to escape the influence of the mother country was precisely the period when the mother country became less "subject to Rome," *i.e.* towards the end of the seventeenth and beginning of the eighteenth centuries, in the age of Voltaire, of Pombal, of Choiseul, and of Mirabeau, of the Encyclopædists, and the persecutors of the Jesuits.

It is not necessary to dilate on this lamentable page of history; it is well known how cleverly the English and Dutch took advantage of passing events to seize on flourishing settlements.

The Spanish and Portuguese colonies resisted separation from the mother country until the time of

Catholics and Colonization.

the departure of the last Jesuit. All the ancient colonies bear traces of their former splendour (in the times when they were subject to Rome).

Neither the Spaniards,[1] the French, nor the Portuguese commenced the work of colonization by proscribing the indigenous inhabitants of the soil; on the contrary, they baptized and educated them, they intermarried with them, and colonized after the manner of Christians. The English and the Dutch have never pursued the same course of action; their practice is to establish houses of business, which are intended to be prosperous and advantageous for thèmselves. In most cases the original Christian settlements founded by the first settlers have been destroyed, and this is particularly noticeable throughout the East.

The history of Christian colonization in India and Japan by St. Francis Xavier is morally more worthy of admiration and materially more wonderful than the expedition of Alexander of Macedonia.

The English and Dutch colonizers have destroyed the work of their predecessors in order to replace it by a system of commercial speculation.

---

[1] With the exception of the Spaniards in the Mexican colonies under Pizarro, and the Portuguese at Goa, who were both strongly condemned by the Church.

T. W. M. Marshall has written an excellent work entitled "Christian Missions," and we know of no treatise on political or social economy which gives more complete information as to the true riches of Christian nations, and on the conditions of civilization amongst the nations that are "seated in the darkness and shadow of death."

In the year 1858, at a meeting of Protestant missionaries, Mr. Crawford, ex-governor of Singapore, made the following statement: "In the Philippine Islands alone, the Spaniards converted several millions of natives, and therefrom resulted an enormous amelioration of their social condition." (*See* "Times," 2nd December, 1858.)

Sir Henry Ellis, a staunch Protestant, confesses in his "Journal of an Embassy to China" (chap. viii. page 442), that great praise is due to the Spaniards for *the foundation of schools throughout the whole of the colony*, and for their incessant efforts to propagate Christian doctrines and practices *by the diffusion of Christian instruction*.

The influence of the clergy in the Philippine Islands, notwithstanding that the Spaniards were in a very small proportion to the natives, is attested by numerous writers. Sir John Bowring, a man who has no leanings

Catholics and Colonization.

towards Catholicism, wrote in 1859: "The Catholic clergy exercise an influence which would appear magical, if it were not regarded by partisans as divine."

In the "Recollections of Manilla," Mr. Robert MacMicking, a zealous Scotch Presbyterian, speaks thus of the Philippine Islands, where he resided for many years:—

"The nations were not subdued by ordinary warrior knights, but by the soldiers of the cross, by priests who inflamed them with their own zeal and ardour for the cause of Christ."

He states that the suppression of the Jesuits (who were banished from the Islands in 1768), had the most disastrous consequences for commerce and agriculture.

"The Church," he proceeds to say, "has for a long period proved that she is the most simple and efficacious instrument for the preservation of order and good government, since through her means people are taught to read at least books of devotion.

The inhabitants of Manilla serving on board their vessels are generally able to sign their names, which is very often not the case with the English sailors in the Philippine Islands.

There are very few Indians who do not know how to read, and this satisfactory result has been obtained in a country entirely given up to the dominion of the clergy and colonized by Spaniards, in a country without an education league and without any form of compulsory instruction.

The original missionaries penetrated to places where soldiers could only venture fully armed; the sword in this case may be said to have given way to the toga, and this with the best of results in the matter of subduing savage races to Christianity and introducing among them arts and civilization. Hundreds and thousands of these wild tribes are now peaceful cultivators of the soil, having learnt from the missionaries the art of tilling the ground, instead of subsisting as hitherto on the products of the chase and in a continued state of mutual hostility."

M. de Laveleye brings forward an example to support his assertion that Catholic countries no longer colonize, which is as follows:[1]—

"The Comte de Beauvoir arrives at Canton. There he sees the Islet of Sha-Myen, ceded to France and England, situated in the midst of the river. The traveller is struck with the contrast between the part ceded to England and that which belongs to France. In six years' time (1867) there have sprung up a little English village, a Protestant Church, a cricket-ground, a training-ground for race-horses, and spacious villas. A pathway separates the British from the French territory. On our territory there are clumps of uncultivated trees, filth, stray dogs, cats, and moles, but not a single house."

This example does not appear to have been well selected, for we presume the Liége professor does not consider English merchants who go to Canton for the sake of doing a good stroke of business as colonizers.

If the cricket-ground belongs to Protestant mis-

[1] See "*Voyage autour du Monde*," vol. ii. p. 247.

sionaries, we think he might find an object more worthy of admiration.

The French missionaries in China have no time to indulge in such sports: they go into the interior of the country to preach the gospel and colonize the natives, in which attempts they frequently suffer martyrdom. It might be well to contrast this passage with the following:[1]—

"Though it is sad to see from Singapore onwards the poverty of French commerce, the general impression is not so hopeless; it is true that England, the Queen of the Seas, is the material sovereign of the Asiatic Empires, both on account of her colossal trade, and because she imports her cottons, and exports fabulous quantities of tea and silk; but, nevertheless, France is the country of ideas, and these ideas are introduced even into the midst of the most unfrequented parts of China.

Let us assist and support with all our power this moral, inexhaustible, and life-giving force, enhanced as it is by the purity and the poverty of its agents, made illustrious by the blood of its martyrs, and strengthened by its holy faith."

We quote the following remarkable passage[2] from the work of a well-known European statesman and diplomatist, Baron Hübner, late Austrian Ambassador in Paris, who begins by the assertion that it is possible

[1] *See* Java, Siam, Canton, "*Voyage autour du Monde,*" p. 438, 9th edition.

[2] *See* "*Promenade autour du Monde,*" by Baron Hübner, vol. ii. p. 233. Translated by Lady Herbert of Lea.

for a nation to be great and powerful without possessing any vocation for colonizing, according to the modern acceptation of the word.

"What is the meaning of colonization? Is it merely the clearing of the soil? In that case the colonies of Louis XIV. in Canada will bear comparison with the most flourishing colonies of any nation in the world. Is it the task of working the soil for the profit of the emigrants? In that case the English doubtless deserve the palm which all the world gives them.

But if we understand by colonization the art of carrying civilization into the hearts of the native population whose territory is occupied, then the Portuguese and Spaniards of the sixteenth and seventeenth centuries would appear to be the first colonizers of the world.

History written by men not at all impartial, has tarnished (and justly, if the facts that are recorded really took place) the reputation of some of the Spanish and Portuguese conquerors, and accused them of unheard-of acts of cruelty and oppression. Even those who were praised for their moderation are said to have made use of means that the spirit of our time would disapprove. But these kingdoms beyond the seas were rich and prosperous, and the capitals of the *presidencias* became the centres of civilization.

The natives flocked into them and took back to their homes with the light of Christianity (though perhaps feeble and uncertain) the ideas, customs, and practices (though very imperfect also) of the civilized world, which effected a real and lasting improvement in their social condition.

Witnesses of undoubted veracity, travellers like Alexander von Humboldt, visited the Spanish colonies at the beginning of the present century, that is to say, at a time when Spain had long descended from her status as a first-class power, and speak with admiration of the organization she had left behind, of the regularity of the administrative service in these colonies, of the security and order which reigned there, and of the wisdom of the colonial laws, drawn up and codified under the reigns of the Philips. The court of Madrid drew from its transatlantic possessions treasures of gold and precious stones, but in return the mother country gave her blood. The constant emigration, which finally exhausted Spain, is in fact one of the principal causes of the rapid decline of this noble and chivalrous nation. To this day, in many districts, the young men expatriate themselves in a body. In the provinces of the north, and especially in the Asturias, only old men and women are to be found ; all the able-bodied men have gone to the Havannah, Peru, or to Rio de la Plata.

When traversing the hamlets buried in the gorges of the mountains of Cantabria, I used to see notices put up in every direction, announcing the departure of emigrant ships from Santander, Gijon, and Ribadisella, for Cuba and South America, all, according to the announcements, provided with surgeons and chaplains. Alas ! both one and the other are necessary, for in these passages the mortality is awful. Every one of these emigrants (and formerly even more so than now) becomes, unknown to himself, an agent for civilization.

Wherever the Spaniards have reigned we find Indian tribes who have embraced Christianity, and adopted to a certain extent the manners and customs of European nations.

The greater part of the politicians who figure at the head of the various republics are of Indian origin.

I have had for colleagues Red Indians of the purest breed, and I have seen ladies of the same complexion, elegantly dressed by French dressmakers, expatiating on the delights of Madame Patti's singing.

I do not cite these individuals as models of statesmen, or these fair critics as great authorities in music, but the fact is none the less significant as being a result of Spanish colonization.

Can as much be said for the English? Evidently not. I set aside all question of India, which I have not yet visited, but everywhere else, especially in North America, the contact of the Anglo-Saxon race with semi-barbarous natives is fatal to the latter. They either adopt the vices of the Europeans, whilst inwardly hating and avoiding them, or become gradually extinct, but in any case they remain what they previously were—savages.

Comparisons of this sort are, however, of little use; it is better to give to each nation its due share of praise and blame."

Further on Baron Hübner writes thus :—

"France is rich enough to pay for her glory, her ideas, her fancies, and sometimes even for her faults and mistakes. Since the days of Louis XIV. she has made a point of being always to the fore, and striking all nations with the prestige of her greatness. The pursuit of this line of policy imposes upon her in these distant regions, sacrifices which are little in harmony with the material interests of her traders, but such a consideration is scarcely ever permitted to stand as an impediment in her path.

She has undertaken the civilizing mission of protecting her co-religionists in every latitude. We will not inquire too minutely into motives which may not be purely religious, but it must be admitted the consequences following from such a course of action have been, and are still productive of great services to humanity.

In the world of ideas, the French are the most expansive people in the universe; it is the French who, as a nation, communicate to the world at large, both for good and evil, their ideas, tastes, and fashions.

To a greater degree than any other nation the French dislike leaving their country, which accounts for the small number of emigrants amongst their population.

French emigrants are the least numerous everywhere, and even those one does meet with are not (saving honourable exceptions) the brightest specimens of their nation. The truth is, France offers to her children space and means wherewith to support them, to arrive at a comfortable independence, and occasionally to riches, and the highest offices of the State.

Those who quit her shores rarely find beyond them the fortune which they have disdained to seek at home. Side by side with these emigrants, who are not always successful, there are others, who while living and acting in comparative obscurity, surround themselves in their distant country with a crown of imperishable glory.

In China, as in every other foreign land, wherever the French flag is seen floating over the building of a consulate, there appears in its neighbourhood the spire of a church, and by its side a convent, school, and hospital.

There the intellects of the native inhabitants are being enlightened by civilization, and human hearts by faith; there the wounds of both souls and bodies are healed, miseries are alleviated, and the apostolic virtues of charity and self-denial are practised.

The missionaries and sisters of charity are not always French; Italy, Spain, Belgium, and other countries have furnished their contingent, but the great majority of these Christian heroes and heroines are the sons and daughters of France, and France is the country that shields them with her powerful protection."[1]

No modern writer is more trustworthy as regards colonization than M. X. Marmier, from whose last in-

[1] "*Promenade autour du Monde,*" p. 247 and following.

teresting work on France and her colonies,[1] we take the following quotation:—

"A succession of disastrous wars and deplorable treaties deprived us of the greater part of our ancient possessions, but we have left behind us a lasting mark.

A distinguished English writer, Anthony Trollope, recently visited the Antilles, and witnessed the persistency of the attachment to France in those islands formerly subject to her, the government of which had not lasted without interruption for centuries, but only for a few years.

Hayti, Tobago, Santa Lucia, and Trinidad are especially remarkable in this way, the latter island having been originally occupied by the Spaniards, then by the English, taken by the French, and again handed over to the Spaniards, from whom it was in turn seized and re-occupied by the English.

What language, says Trollope, prevails in this island, occupied by an English governor, an English administrative council, an English garrison, and large and important English mercantile houses of business?

Neither English nor Spanish, but French alone!

The whole population is French in language, customs, and religion. Trollope also informs his readers that the island possesses a resident Catholic Bishop who receives an annual stipend from the Government of Great Britain, and that the whole of it is distributed in charity.

At St. Vincent there is yet another example to be found of the attraction exercised by our emigrants. When the English seized the island, the Caraïbes, who occupied a portion of it, rose in a body three different times to expel them, and to demand the return of the French, whose rule they loved."

[1] "*En Pays Lointains*," par X. Marmier, de l'Académie Française. Hachette, Paris.

This same clever academician has collected together a mass of similar statements, all tending to demonstrate the following arguments:—

"It is often stated that France is unable to colonize, but is such really the case?

The history of our colonies is one of the noblest and most attractive pages of our national history, and has been often recounted at different times and in different places with great learning and eloquence.

I make no pretence of stating anything new, but in collecting the impressions of my journey, and in adding to it recent studies, I only wish to point out the characteristic features and individual qualities of colonization with which France has always been endowed, such especially as courage in undertakings, generosity in victory, and dignity in misfortune.

Other nations may have more brilliant victories to vaunt, but none that will prove so durable or lasting."

The testimony of M. X. Marmier ought to carry as much weight as that of M. Thiers, who forty years ago scoffed at the future of the railway system, and who remained to the day of his death a strong opponent of free-trade.

The colonies of French missionaries in this century recall the glory of the great *Descupradores*, of the Iberian peninsula; and Algeria, colonized by the French during the last forty-five years, can well bear comparison with the places conquered by the Anglo-Saxons since the reign of Louis XV.

Father Marquette was the first person to discover the Meschacabe, which was afterwards traversed to its source by Robert Lasalle, in order to take possession of Louisiana in the name of France, where Bienville subsequently founded the city of New Orleans.

Quebec owes its foundation to another Frenchman of the name of Champlain.

We quote from Marmier the following account of the founding of Montreal:—

"In the year 1641 two small vessels left La Rochelle for Canada. On board one of them was a saintly woman, Mdlle. Mause, from the town of Langres, who sacrificed a brilliant position in her own country to devote her life to works of charity in the wild and barbarous regions of North America. On board the other was a man of noble birth from the province of Champagne, M. de Maisonneuve, and with him a priest and a few soldiers and labourers, making in all thirty persons.

These travellers reached Quebec in the month of August, where the inhabitants implored them to remain.

The town was at that time composed of only 200 souls, and thirty good people would have been a valuable reinforcement.

M. de Maisonneuve being pledged to proceed to Hochelaga, was unable to comply with the request.

It was in vain that he was warned of the dangers to which he would be exposed in landing on an island occupied by a powerful tribe of Indians, with only a handful of soldiers ; he always replied he had not come to deliberate on such a question, but to carry out the project he had undertaken, and that if there were at Hochelaga as many Iroquois as trees on the plain, his honour and sense of duty would still oblige him to proceed.

In the month of October he reached the shores of Hochelaga, and immediately constructed a few huts and a chapel of wood.

Mdlle. Mause organized in the same spot a hospital, and a sister of charity from Troyes established an institution of free education for young girls.

A few tents situated in the middle of the forest, a chapel of wood, with leaves for its roof, and a bell suspended from a fir-tree, a hospital for the sick, and a school for the poor; such were the first beginnings of the great city of Montreal, which now contains more than 80,000 inhabitants. No one can pretend that the Anglo-Saxons or Dutch settlers acted in a similar way.

One of the jewels of the colonial empire of Great Britain is the island of Mauritius, called by its pacific conqueror, the Chevalier de Fougères, commander of the 'Triton,' 'Isle de France.'

This brave officer erected on the shore a cross, decorated with *fleurs-de-lys*, and the following inscription :—'*Jubet hic Gallia stare Crucem.*'"

We have no hesitation in dilating on remembrances like these, since they are more glorious for France than all the immortal conquests of 1789, or all the victories of the First Empire.

Jacques Cartier, who with two small vessels made the circuit of Newfoundland, to ascend the river St. Lawrence, thus describes the commencement of the expedition, which we quote in order to show the spirit in which it was undertaken :—

"On Sunday, the Feast of Pentecost, by the order of the captain, and with common goodwill, all on board went to confession, and together received holy communion in the cathedral church of St. Malo, after which we all presented ourselves in the choir of the above-named church before the bishop of the diocese, and received his special benediction."

Father Marquette, the discoverer of the river Mississippi, wrote the following admirable words :—

"If the voyage had had no other result than the salvation of one soul, I should have considered my labours well rewarded."

The whole history of the colonization of North America by the *Yankees* does not present one figure so noble as that of Montcalm, the hero of French Canada.

It is most probable that if Spain, Portugal, and France had not suffered themselves to be weakened and despoiled of their rights, by the Cæsarism of the Bourbons, and by the political doctrines of 1789, called liberal, they would be to-day what they were formerly, and what they may yet again become, the first colonizers of the world. The masterpiece of the colonial policy of modern England is India, but even here in the metropolis of their Eastern Empire (Calcutta) the English only follow the example of France in the secondary matter of commercial interests.

Lord Macaulay[1] writes thus :—

[1] "Critical and Historical Essays," by Lord Macaulay.

"The man who first saw that it was possible to found an European empire on the ruins of the Mogul monarchy was Dupleix.

His restless, capacious, and inventive mind had formed this scheme, at a time when the ablest servants of the English company were busied only about invoices and bills of lading.

The arts both of war and policy which a few years later were employed with such signal success by the English, were first understood and practised by this ingenious and inspiring Frenchman. He saw that the natives of India, under European commanders, might be formed into armies such as Frederick or Saxe would be proud to command."

If it be true that no nations who are subject to Rome any longer colonize, what nations may truly be said to colonize?

Lutheran Prussia and Calvinistic Switzerland certainly do not.

Let us examine as to the part taken by England, Holland, and the United States of America.

These latter nations have undoubtedly distinguished themselves in our day by their practical and general knowledge, and by their energetic adherence to a certain line of commercial and colonial policy, a line that must, however, be carefully distinguished from the civilizing and Christian work of colonization, according to its proper and original definition.

The present colonial policy of England is neither Protestant, Catholic, nor anti-Catholic; it has for its one object the mercantile interest of Great Britain; the doctrines of Adam Smith are practised, without, however, excluding the simultaneous application by individuals of the great religious principles of colonization formerly employed with so much success by the Spaniards, the French, and the Portuguese.

The greater number of the colonies at present in the possession of England are recent acquisitions, formerly in the hands of the French, the Dutch, and the Portuguese. Great Britain no longer possesses New England (one of her rare creations), a colony which she may be said to have founded in spite of herself.

New England was originally a colony composed of fugitive malcontents, misanthropes, and sectarians, all voluntary exiles from their native land (who would willingly have retained them had she been able) by reason of the religious persecutions of the Stuarts.

The code of New England was conceived in the most ferocious spirit, and was enforced with relentless severity. The Puritans of New England outdid in their fierce intolerance those whose milder tyranny had compelled them to seek relief in exile. A simple extract from the law passed at Plymouth on the 14th October, 1657, will be sufficient to display the mild and Christian policy of those Protestant civilizers, who themselves had suffered for conscience sake :—

"It is further enacted that if any Quaker or Quakers shall presume, after they have once suffered what the law requireth, to come into this jurisdiction, every such male Quaker shall, for the first offence, have one of his ears cut off, and for the second offence have the other ear cut off," &c. "Every female Quaker shall be severely whipped, and for the second offence shall have her tongue bored through with a hot iron," &c. &c.

The contrast offered by the different policy pursued by Catholic and Puritan colonists should put to shame those who are so lavish in their accusations of Catholic persecution. When the Catholics had power, they proclaimed the broadest toleration, and fullest liberty to every sect of Christians. In Catholic Maryland there was no ear-cropping, or boring of tongues with hot pokers. Such exhibitions of brotherly love were reserved for the Puritans of Plymouth. The illustrious name of Lord Baltimore is closely allied with toleration in unfurling the banner of civil and religious liberty upon the continent of North America. The disfranchised friends of prelacy from Massachusetts and the Puritans from Virginia were welcomed to equal liberty of conscience and political rights in the Catholic province of Maryland. These halcyon days did not long continue, for when the Protestants got the upper hand, they persecuted the Catholics, who had extended liberty to all. Cardinal Manning, Archbishop of Westminster, in a reply to a pamphlet by Mr. Gladstone on the Vatican Council of 1870, relates the history of the foundation of Maryland in the following words:[1]—

"Lord Baltimore, who had been Secretary of State under James I. in 1633, emigrated to the American plantations, where, through Lord Strafford's influence, he had obtained a grant of land.

He was accompanied by men of all minds, who agreed chiefly in the one desire to leave behind them the miserable religious conflicts which then tormented England. They named their new country Maryland, and there they settled. The oath of the governor was in these terms: '*I will not, by myself or any other, directly or indirectly, molest any person professing to believe in Jesus Christ, for or in respect of religion.*'

Lord Baltimore invited the Puritans of Massachusetts, who, like himself, had renounced their country for conscience sake, to come to Maryland.

In 1649, when active persecution had sprung up again in England, the council of Maryland, on the 21st of April, passed this statute: 'And whereas the forcing of the conscience in matters of religion hath frequently fallen out to be of dangerous consequences in the commonwealth where it has been practised, and for the more quiet and peaceable government of the province and the better to preserve mutual love and amity among

---

[1] *See* "Vatican Decrees in their bearing on Civil Allegiance." By Henry Edward, Archbishop of Westminster. P. 91. Longmans.

the inhabitants, no person within the province professing to believe in Jesus Christ shall be any ways troubled, molested, or discountenanced for his or her religion, or in the free exercise thereof.'

The Episcopalians and Protestants fled from Virginia into Maryland. Such was the commonwealth, founded by a Catholic upon the broad moral law I have laid down—that faith is an act of the will, and that to force men to profess what they do not believe, is contrary to the law of God, and that to generate faith by force is morally impossible. It was by conviction of the reason and persuasion of the will that the world-wide unity of faith and communion were slowly built up among the nations.

When once shattered, nothing but conviction and persuasion can restore it. Lord Baltimore was surrounded by a multitude scattered by the great wreck of the Tudor persecutions.

He knew that God alone could build them up again into unity, but that the equity of charity might enable them to protect and help each other and to promote the common weal. I cannot refrain from continuing the history. The Puritan commonwealth in England brought on a Puritan revolution in Maryland. They acknowledged Cromwell and disfranchised the whole Catholic population. Liberty of conscience was declared, but to the exclusion of popery, prelacy, and licentiousness of opinion. Penal laws came in due course. Quakers in Massachusetts for the first offence lost one ear, for the second the other, and for the third had their tongue seared with a red-hot iron. Women were whipped and men hanged for religion."

England has been severely punished for her intolerant spirit by the loss of the only countries she could (before the sixteenth century) truly lay a claim to have colonized by peopling with her own sons.

The punishment has been the more severe from the fact that she has had to witness the founding of a rival nation speaking the same Anglo-Saxon tongue, upon the territories that formerly belonged to her.

The Dutch at present are not in possession of a single colony of their own creation—that is to say, of any colony enjoying the institutions, the manners, the customs, and the religion of the mother country.

Their Indian settlement is an enormous counting-house of industry and commerce, protected by a powerful army; they seek their fortunes in India, and return to Europe to enjoy the benefit of their income at the Hague, Amsterdam, or Brussels, but they do not colonize in the Spanish, Portuguese, or French sense of the word.

We make no reproaches, but we wish to point out the difference between the Catholic ideas of colonization and those entertained by the various non-Catholic sects.

The United States, actuated by the political genius of the Anglo-Saxon race, owes its extraordinary and unprecedented development chiefly to immigration.

We have not at present before us the complete statistics of the wonderful westward movement of the

European nations, but we entertain no doubt that one of the principal causes of the greatness of North America consists in the large importation of Catholics.

England has frequently boasted that she is the mother-land of America, and yet she has little claim even to this. The majority of English-speaking emigrants that have flocked there in such large numbers during the last thirty or forty years are Irish; but to go farther back in history, the first European who went to America was Christopher Columbus, an Italian; the second, Americus Vespucci, a Portuguese; the third, Sebastian Cabot, a Spaniard; and yet these persons are reckoned the founders of America.

Was it not the Dutch who settled New York, and the Swedes Jersey? Was it not the Danes who settled Delaware, and the Huguenots South Carolina, the Spanish Florida, and the French Louisiana? The very capital in which Congress is held was presented by Carroll, an Irishman, and by careful examination it will be seen that from the lakes to the gulf, and from ocean to ocean, there is not ten per cent. of English blood in the veins of the people. '

From the Grand Duchy of Luxembourg, in many instances came whole villages, with their parish priest, burgomaster, and schoolmaster.

All the new Western States of the Union are peopled by Catholics, and in order to be convinced of the importance of the Catholic population of the United States, it is sufficient to consider the ecclesiastical hierarchy which has sprung up during the last half century, and now numbers forty episcopal sees.

The French Catholic population is increasing in English Canada, where Irish Catholics (the true colonizing missionaries of Great Britain) have settled in great numbers.

In Australia, New Zealand, and Tasmania the number of the hierarchy is evident proof of the numerous Catholic population. We do not profess to claim exclusively for Catholics the privilege (often mixed with bitterness) of emigration, but our impression is that in the great colonizing movement which this age has witnessed among the Anglo-Saxon races, Catholic civilization holds the first rank.

We must not omit one instance of Catholic colonization that has occurred within the last few years. After the dispersion of the Papal Zouaves consequent on the seizure of Rome by the Italian Government, a portion of that body who were from Canada obtained lands in the forests of their native country, cleared the ground, and erected a small village which is rapidly rising into a town and bringing the adjacent territory into cultivation. This small colony has already prospered beyond all expectation, and is ruled in the spirit of true Christianity, such as was witnessed in the early days of the Church. The village bears the name of Piopolis, in honour of the venerated Pontiff Pius IX.

Much might be said on the question of the British government in India, did this work permit of details, but no one can dispute the energy, intelligence, and courage that have been displayed by English statesmen in their dealings with that empire.

It is no doubt desirable that India should remain in the hands of Great Britain, for though the English may not have fulfilled the duties of Christian colonizers in the true sense of the term, they have nevertheless not prevented others from doing it for them, and have always acted as an obstacle to the terrible anarchy that would otherwise exist amongst the natives.

The courage, discipline, and bravery of English troops throughout this immense empire, eight times as vast, and six times as thickly populated as the United Kingdom of Great Britain, and kept in hand by a small body of Europeans, certainly presents a spectacle which cannot fail to reflect credit on the present polity of the English monarchy.

Economists may admire the vast network of railways and telegraphs with which the administration of the governors has covered the country, and financiers may calculate the dividends that the English residents annually receive after a final settlement of accounts; but as far as we are concerned, we think the results obtained by the old colonization of the Portuguese and the French, and the actual present condition of the Spanish colony of the Philippine Islands are more worthy of praise.

The action of the English, both in India and in the Chinese seas, is poor in comparison with the heroic conquests of St. Francis Xavier in the sixteenth century, when, armed with the Gospel and the crucifix, he traversed the country which practically became the scene of his martyrdom, and whose annals are written in the blood of the missionaries in Asia.

The work of the propagation of the faith (by which thousands are made Christians), the most colossal instrument of colonization known in history, was originally the idea of a poor servant at Lyons, who formed the conception of a large number of persons who should contribute a certain amount weekly.

This simple idea, blessed by the Church, has been developed; and the money thus collected serves to send to all parts of the earth men who become instruments of civilization, and whose blood possesses the marvellous property of fertilizing the nations who commit the crime of shedding it. "*Sanguis martyrum semen Christianorum*" ("The blood of martyrs is the seed of Christianity").

We are aware that missionaries are sent out also by the various Protestant sects, and we have no wish to criticize the acts of men who work in a spirit of devotion and self-denial; but we must be permitted to make the remark that the results of Protestant missions, however worthy of respect in the intention of their promoters, cannot be placed on a par with the striking results obtained by the Catholic apostolate.[1]

Father Smet, an eminent Jesuit (whose life and letters have been published by Father Deynoodt), was by himself more powerful amongst the Red Indians than the government of the United States.

His charity, inspired by his faith, had been the means of subduing many tribes, and when the government wished to obtain anything from the ancient

---

[1] *See* the writings of Cardinal Wiseman on "*the unfruitfulness of Protestant missions to the heathen.*"

possessors of the soil, they were obliged to turn to this Belgian minister of the gospel. The companions of this civilizer, this veritable doctor of colonization, were all Belgian priests.

There is at present a special American foundation in the University of Louvain, instituted forthe expres s purpose of sending out missionaries to America.

The Bengal mission is in the hands of Belgian Jesuits, who possess a flourishing college in the presidency, and render more service to the English authorities than a whole regiment of infantry.

The learned Father Carbonelle, secretary of the Scientific Society of Brussels, has but recently returned from this mission.

The soil on which large numbers of these men have sacrificed their health, in this work of civilization, is rendered illustrious by the labours of ancient Jesuits, that indefatigable body, who so perseveringly seek to repair what has been destroyed by want of civilization and the spirit of error.

Professor David Forbes, F.R.S., relates how in one of his scientific expeditions in South America, he fell into the hands of a body of Indians, who would have scalped him had he not been delivered from them by some black men called Jesuits. These men were engaged in the work of the evangelization of the savages, about a hundred miles from the shores of the Atlantic, at the foot of the Cordilleras, where for the love of Christ they lived in the midst of the heathen, and spent their lives in educating and instructing them. Professor Forbes declares that they are everywhere treated with respect, and that in his estimation they are the greatest colonizers of the day.

Father Verbiest, late chaplain to the Military Academy at Brussels, wishing to carry the word of truth to the country where his compatriot the Franciscan John of Ruysbroek had toiled in bygone days, laid the foundation of a mission in Mongolia, and met with his death in a desert between the 40th and 50th degree of latitude. This work of civilization is still living and productive.

We must not omit to make mention of the religious congregations of women who go out in large numbers to instruct the young, both in Africa, Asia, America, and Australia.

The mother house of Notre Dame de Namur in Belgium has alone founded more than twenty stations in the most varied latitudes.

Facts like these speak volumes on the question of colonization, and we feel no hesitation in asking the unprejudiced of all creeds, whether it is reasonable to make the assertion that Catholics do not colonize, and whether those who make the assertion can have rightly studied the question of colonization?

CHAPTER V.

CATHOLICISM AND CIVIL LIBERTY.

Persecution, revolution, and tyranny in Protestant and Catholic countries—Moral characteristics of the great French Revolution—Civil liberty in Italy—In Belgium—Meaning of the word political liberty in the mouths of the Neo-Protestant school of Continental liberals—Their object in preaching Protestantism in Catholic countries—Essays of Quinet and Eugène Sue—Discussion of liberty amongst Continental liberals.

ERSECUTION has not only been more generally practised by Protestants than by Catholics, but it has been more warmly defended and supported by the former than by the latter.

Bergier defies Protestants to mention a single town in which their predecessors, on becoming masters of it, tolerated a single Catholic.

Rousseau, who was educated a Protestant, says,[1] that "the Reformation was intolerant from its cradle, and its authors universally persecutors."

Bayle, a celebrated Calvinist, has published much the same thing.

The Huguenot minister Jurieu acknowledges the fact "that Geneva, Switzerland, the various principalities of Germany, England, Scotland, Sweden, and Denmark had all employed the power of the State to abolish Popery, and establish the Reformation."[2]

The moderate Melancthon wrote a book[3] in defence of religious persecution. Calvin was its great champion, and Beza, who succeeded him, wrote a folio work in defence of it.[4]

John Knox advocates it in all his writings.[5]

Edwin Sandys, Bishop of London, published a book in vindication of it.[6]

James I. was repeatedly urged by parliament to enforce the laws against Catholics with greater rigour,

---

[1] "*Lettres de la Mont.*"

[2] "*Tab. Lett.*," quoted by Bossuet, avertiss., p. 625.

[3] "*De Hæretecis puniendis a civili magistratu, &c.*, a Theod. Beza."

[4] "*De Hæret. puniend.*," Beza.

[5] *See* Milner's "End of Religious Controversy," p. 439.

[6] Ger. Brandt, "Hist. Reform.," abridg., vol. i. p. 234.

and Archbishop Abbott warned him against the sin of toleration. (*See* Rushworth's collection, vol. i. p. 144.)

Archbishop Usher and eleven Irish bishops presented an address to Charles I. against toleration, in which they declared that to give toleration to Papists was a grievous sin. (*See* Leland's "Hist. of Ireland," vol. ii. p. 482, and Neal's "Hist.," vol. ii. p. 469.)

The Presbyterian divines assembled at Sion College condemned as an error "the doctrine of toleration," under the abused term, as they expressed it, "of liberty of conscience."[1]

James II. was deposed by the English nation because he wished that all his subjects should enjoy the same privileges; and to the present day, the mere fact of a man's being a Catholic is sufficient to make his return to Parliament in any English county almost an impossibility.

Dr. Milner says, with great justice, that when Catholic States and princes persecuted Protestants, it was done in favour of an ancient religion, which had been established in their country perhaps a thousand or fifteen hundred years, and which had long preserved the peace, order, and morality of their respective subjects, and when at the same time

[1] "History of Churches of England and Scotland," vol. iii.

they clearly saw that any attempt to alter this religion would unavoidably produce disorders and sanguinary contests among them.

Protestants, on the contrary, everywhere persecuted on behalf of new systems, in opposition to the established laws of the Church and of the respective States.

Nothing was ever more unfounded than the notion that Protestantism is favourable to freedom of conscience, or that Protestants were not persecutors.

Protestants not only persecuted Catholics, but they persecuted each other to the death.

In Scotland the Reformation may be said to have begun by the assassination of Cardinal Beaton, to which Knox was a party, and to which Fox, in his "Acts and Monuments," says the murderers were instigated by the Spirit of God. "With such indecent haste," says Robertson, "did the very persons who had just escaped ecclesiastical tyranny proceed to imitate the example" (Robertson's "History of Scotland"). See also the answer of the Presbytery to the King and Council in 1596, concerning the Catholic Earls of Huntley, Erroll, &c., which declared that the civil power could not spare them, as they were guilty of idolatry, a crime punishable by death.

In France it is well known that wherever the Huguenots carried their victorious arms against their sovereign, they prohibited the exercise of the Catholic religion, slaughtered the priests, and burnt the churches and convents (Maimbourg, "Hist. Calvinism").

One of their own writers, Nicholas Froumanteau, confesses that in the single province of Dauphiny they killed 256 priests and 112 monks ("*Liv. de France*").

In these scenes the famous Baron des Adrets signalized his notions of Protestant civilization by forcing the Catholic prisoners to jump from the towers upon the pikes of his soldiers, and by compelling his own children to wash their hands in the blood of the Catholics.

In the Low Countries it was an ordinary thing for the Calvinists to assault the clergy in the discharge of their functions. Wherever Vandermeck and Sonoi, both of them lieutenants of the Prince of Orange, carried their arms, they uniformly put to death in cold blood all the priests and religious they could lay hands on, as at Dort, Middlebourg, Delft, &c. ("*Hist. Ref. des Pays Bas*," by the Protestant minister, De Brandt).

Feller, a celebrated biographer, states that Vandermeck slaughtered more unoffending Catholics in the year 1752 than Alva executed Protestants during his whole government.

Monsieur Keroux, a Protestant writer in "*L'Abrégé de l'Histoire de la Hollande*," draws a frightful picture of the barbarities committed against the Catholic peasants of North Holland. Amongst the more illustrious foreign Protestants who suffered death by the violence of other Protestants may be mentioned the names of Servetus, Gentilis, Felix Mans, Rotman, and Barnevelt.

In England during the reign of Edward VI. many Protestant dissenters were condemned and burnt. (*See* Stow's "Annals.") During the reign of Elizabeth large numbers of persons suffered torture and death for their religious opinions. Full descriptions of those who were thus punished may be found in the works of Stow, Brandt, Collier, Neal, &c.

Under James I., Legat and Wrightman were publicly executed for Arianism, and under Charles I. the dissenters complained loudly of their sufferings, and particularly that four of their number—Leighton, Burton, Prynne, and Bastwick—were cropped of their ears and set in the pillory. (*See* Limborch's "History of Inquisition," Neal, &c.)

When the dissenters got the upper hand they continued to put Catholics to death and treated the Episcopalians with great severity, at the same time appointing days of humiliation and fasting to beg God's pardon for not being more intolerant. (*See* Neal's "History of Puritans," "History of Churches of England and Scotland.")

The editor of De Laune's "Plea for Nonconformists" says that this writer was one of 8,000 Protestant dissenters who perished in prison in the single reign of Charles II., merely for dissenting from the Church of England as by law established. For the capital punishment and other sufferings of the Quakers our readers may refer to Penn's "Life of George Fox."

The history of the persecutions perpetrated by the Established Church of England upon Catholics on the one hand and Protestant dissenters on the other, is one of the blackest in the page of time.

Protestant countries can lay no claim to be exempt from anarchy and revolution.

To begin with, neither Switzerland nor the United States of America can be considered harbours of refuge against them; the latter, having but lately emerged from the effects of a terrible civil war which may break out again at any moment, has suffered much from discontent amongst the masses, and was, but a short time ago, a prey to the horrors of bloodshed owing to a general strike of railway labourers throughout the whole country.

The former is full of the elements of anarchy and discontent. The different Swiss cantons are perpetually at variance, although the common object of self-defence is able to silence many differences.

Since the Reformation, Switzerland has had its full share of insurrection and revolution, and at the present moment offers an example of a tyrannical government and a discontented population.

Witness the arbitrary expulsion of Monsignor Mermillod, Vicar Apostolic of Geneva and Bishop of Hebron, in the year 1872; the forcible ejection of Catholic priests and people from their lawful churches, and the intrusion of State-appointed apostate clergy in the Jura,[1] in spite of repeated petitions against such proceedings.

---

[1] M. Loyson, an apostate French Carmelite, was installed by the civil authorities of Geneva as curé of the parish, in defiance of the wishes of the people, who at once withdrew from his ministrations. The sequel is amusing. M. Loyson became disgusted with the situation, his followers being composed of atheists and freethinkers, and threw up the post, declaring that he did so because those who had appointed him were neither liberals nor Catholics.

In Geneva a Government clique, composed of Protestants, Jews, and Atheists, have seized on all the ecclesiastical property, even that which had been originally given by private individuals,[1] and in Lausanne they have made several attempts to upset the whole machinery of ecclesiastical legislation.

Till near the close of the seventeenth century Switzerland was distracted by dissensions, and in the year 1703 the whole of the Catholic and Protestant cantons were openly arrayed against each other. From this period to the close of the eighteenth century internal discord paved the way for external aggression, and rendered it an easy prey to the great French Republic.

The Dutch have had many more periods of anarchy than their Belgian neighbours of the same race.

For the space of two centuries Holland was torn asunder by a spirit of faction, and was only saved from the absolutism of the House of Orange by the partial want of success of the Calvinists.

Had these latter been altogether triumphant, Hol-

---

[1] The church of Notre Dame, built by the contributions of Catholics throughout the world, has been forcibly taken possession of by the government and handed over to the sect of Alt-Catholics. These latter are so few in number and so irreligious in practice that they make but little use of it, and it was recently lent for a musical entertainment.

land would have shared the political fate of Sweden, Denmark, and Prussia.

Towards the close of the eighteenth century the troubled state of the country induced the Dutch to seek foreign intervention, and their land was successively occupied by the Prussians, the French, and the English. In 1787 the Prussians were masters of Amsterdam, and openly espoused the cause of the House of Orange.

In 1795 a fellow-soldier of Bernadotte reduced the whole kingdom of Holland to the state of a department of the great French Republic.

Perpetual quarrels between Arminians and Calvinists headed by Arminius and Gomarus distracted the country.

The Protestants of North Germany until the year 1848 were (like the Assyrians or Babylonians) in a state of comparative tranquillity because they were completely crushed under the heel of a civil despotism, the most consummate in the record of modern history.

The Prussian historian Leo declares that the natural result of the Reformation was the increase of power amongst the sovereigns and various rulers throughout Germany, and the destruction of the liberty of the lesser nobles and the peasants.

The Thirty Years' War which devastated Germany was the distinct legacy of the Reformation, and the war of seven years arose from the designs and intrigues of the Prussian sovereigns. Germans against Germans, monarch against monarch in a scramble for territory, and the people indifferent and with no interest at issue, was the spectacle presented in Northern Germany.

The sovereigns made conquests according to the number of their highly-disciplined troops.

War was carried on by them just as players at chess or draughts carry on warfare and calculate the powers and effect of each piece. The military system of the German governments engendered a spirit of interference not only with the labouring class of the community, but with all business and employment.

At the present moment Prussia is in a state of revolutionary ferment, of which no one can foresee the result. Up to the year 1860 socialism hardly existed in Germany; since then it has made rapid strides. In the year 1869 it had six journals that represented its principles; now it has fifty, in addition to almanacs, pamphlets, and flying sheets, which are circulated by hundreds of thousands. Herr Most, a celebrated socialist leader, declared not long ago at a public meeting[1] that church-goers had dwindled into a small minority, and that Christianity was dying out.

The daily papers of the 15th and 16th January, 1877, were loud in their disapproval of the successes of the socialists and democrats at the elections that had then taken place, and expressed their dread at the future that was before them.

From the year 1637 to the year 1720 Denmark was a prey to perpetual war, and from that time has been ground down under a gross form of despotism.

The revolution of 1660 destroyed the despotism of the nobles, but little improvement took place with regard to the great mass of the population.

In the year 1687 the wretched condition of the Danish peasantry was so alarming that a fifth part of the lands formerly cultivated by them was allowed to remain fallow.

In the eighteenth century whole villages disappeared in the abyss of misery, caused by the despotic character of the government.

Sweden cannot be cited as an example of the peace enjoyed by nations that have accepted the Reformation. For the last 300 years she has been a prey to perpetual troubles and revolutions. The an-

[1] *See* "Times," March 22nd, 1878.

archy that Europe has witnessed in modern Spain is as nothing in comparison to the revolutions in Sweden which disposed of two kings, Sigismund and Gustavus IV., and killed three more—Eric XIV., Charles XII., and Gustavus III.

The Swedish people carried the love of sedition to the extent of repudiating their own national dynasty, by handing over their country to a soldier of fortune, who rose from the ranks of the great French Revolution.

The Reformation benefited nobody except the nobility, who practically made royalty subservient to them.

In the year 1680 the States declared that they regarded it as an "absurdity" that the king should be obliged by the statutes to give them a hearing before finally deciding on questions of government. In 1693 the sovereign power was declared to be absolute, and Charles XII. caused the Diet to be told that he would send his boots to preside over its sittings.

After the murder of that amiable freethinker, Swedish liberty, *i.e.* the dominion of the nobles, was re-established, and a series of revolutions followed in rapid succession, concluding with the murder of Gustavus. From that period Sweden became a mass of intrigue and political corruption. Finland was seized upon by Russia, and the kingdom of Sweden found no political rest save in the arms of a French general who deemed that a crown was well worth an abjuration.

We hear a great deal about the blessings which resulted to England from the liberty of the Reformation, but what the Reformation really did was to make England the scene of constantly recurring insurrections and civil wars from the "Pilgrimage of Grace" till the rebellion of 1745, the risings (always justifiable, except it be admitted that Protestant governments are never to be resisted) being always put down with the most ruthless ferocity.

The Reformation cost the Church of England at least half the population of the United Kingdom, and the country her most treasured possession, the United States of America. As a reformation of manners it proved the most complete failure. It was an outbreak of anomia in the first instance, and cruelty and tyranny in its latter stages.

Mr. Froude declares that five or six times as much blood was shed by Queen Elizabeth as by her sister Queen Mary, without so much provocation, as there was no insurrection against her as in the case of

Queen Mary, and yet one is held out to the public as "Bloody Mary," and the other as "good Queen Bess."

From Hallam's "Constitutional History" we quote the following passage:—

"The Church of England, for more than 150 years after the Reformation, continued to be the servile handmaid of monarchy, and the steady enemy of public liberty. The divine right of kings, and the duty of passively obeying them and all their commands, were her favourite tenets. She held them firmly through times of oppression, persecution, and licentiousness; while law was trampled down, while judgment was perverted, while the people were eaten as though they were bread. Once and but once, for a moment and but for a moment, when her own dignity and property were touched, she forgot to practise the submission which she had taught." [1]

Again:—

"By no artifice of ingenuity can the stigma of persecution, the worst blemish of the English Church, be effaced or patched over. When Elizabeth put Ballard and Babington to death, she was not persecuting, nor should we have accused her government of persecution for passing any law, however severe, against overt acts of sedition. But to argue that because a man is a Catholic, he must think it right to murder a heretical sovereign, and that because he thinks it right, he will attempt to do it, and then to found on this conclusion a law for punishing him as if he had done it, is plain persecution." [2]

[1] Macaulay's "Essays," p. 64.   [2] *Ibid.*, p. 59.

Mr. Lecky writes as follows: [1]—

"It would be scarcely possible to conceive a more infamous system of legal tyranny than that which in the eighteenth century crushed every class and almost every interest in Ireland. The Parliament had been deprived of every vestige of independence. The Irish judges might at any time be removed.

Manufacturing and commercial industry had been deliberately crushed for the benefit of English manufacturers, and the country was reduced to such a state of poverty that the government was compelled to borrow £20,000 from a private individual to pay its troops.

At the same time a gigantic and ever-increasing pension-list was drawn up from the scanty resources of the nation, and was expended partly in corrupting its representatives and partly in rewarding foreigners. The mistresses of George I., the Queen-Dowager of Prussia, sister of George II., and the Sardinian ambassador who negotiated the Peace of Paris, were all on the pension-lists.

The Catholics, excluded from almost every possibility of eminence, deprived of their natural leaders, and consigned by the legislature to utter ignorance, soon sank into the condition of broken and dispirited helots.

For the greater part of a century the main object of the legislature was to extirpate a religion by the encouragement of some of the worst, and the punishment of some of the best qualities of our nature.

Its rewards were reserved for the informer, for the hypocrite, for the undutiful son, or for the faithless wife. Its penalties were directed against religious constancy and the honest discharge of ecclesiastical duty.

---

[1] *See* "Leaders of Public Opinion in Ireland," by Lecky, pp. 125, 127. Longmans and Green, 1871.

It is impossible for any Irish Protestant whose mind is not wholly perverted by religious bigotry, to look back without shame and indignation to the penal code. The annals of persecution contain many more sanguinary pages. They contain no instance of a series of laws more deliberately and ingeniously framed to debase their victims, to bribe them in every stage of their life to abandon their convictions, and to sow dissension and distrust within the family circle.

That the Irish Parliament in the last years of William, and in the reigns of his two successors, was one of the most persecuting legislative assemblies that ever sat, cannot reasonably be questioned.

The code of laws inaugurated in the reign of William III. is described by Burke as a code well digested and well disposed in all its parts, a machine of wise and elaborate contrivance, and as well fitted for the oppression, impoverishment, and degradation of a people, and the debasement in them of human nature itself, as ever proceeded from the perverted ingenuity of man.

It was framed by a small minority of the nation for the oppression of the majority, who remained faithful to the religion of their fathers. It was framed by men who boasted that their creed rested upon private judgment, and whose descendants are never weary of declaiming upon the intolerance of Popery, and was in all its parts so strictly a code of religious persecution that any Catholic might be exempted from its operation by simply forsaking his religion."

From Hallam's "Constitutional History" (third edition, vol. i. p. 130) we quote the following passage:—

"Tolerance in religion, it is well known, so unanimously admitted at least verbally in the present century, was seldom considered practicable, much less a matter of right, during the period of the Reformation."

And again :—

"It appears that at the end of the seventeenth century the Irish or Anglo-Irish Catholics could hardly possess above one-sixth or one-seventh of the kingdom. They were still formidable from their numbers and their sufferings, and the victorious party saw no security but in a system of oppression, contained in a series of laws during the reigns of William and Anne, which have scarce a parallel in European history.

No Papist was allowed to keep a school, or teach in any private houses, except the children of the family, and no Papist could be a guardian to any child," &c. &c. &c.

"To have exterminated the Catholics by the sword, or expelled them like the Moriscoes of Spain, would have been little more repugnant to justice and humanity, but incomparably more politic."[1]

From Prendergast's "Cromwellian Settlement" (p. 16) we quote the following :—

"If a Protestant married an Irishwoman, and did not conform to the English religion within one year of the marriage, he sank to the helot-like condition of his wife's people, and was deprived of *all rights*, he became *a constructive Papist*, and was regarded as worse than a born one."

Grattan, in one of his celebrated speeches, said :—

"Civil and religious liberty depends upon political power; the community that has no share directly or indirectly in political power has no security for its political liberty."

[1] Hallam's "Constitutional History," vol. iii. p. 532.

Mr. Freeman, in his work entitled "Growth of the English Constitution,"[1] writes as follows :—

" The old paths have in England ever been the paths of progress ; the ancient custom has ever been to shrink from mere change for the sake of change, but fearlessly to change whenever change was needed. And many of the best changes of later times, many of the most wholesome improvements in our law and constitution, have been only the casting aside of innovations which crept in in modern and evil times. They have been the calling up again, in an altered garb, of principles as old as the days when we get our first sight of our forefathers in the German forests.

Changed as it is in all outward forms and circumstances, the England in which we live has, in its true life and spirit, far more in common with the England of the earliest times than it has with the England of days far nearer to our own. In many a wholesome act of modern legislation we have gone back, wittingly or unwittingly, to the earliest principle of our race. We have advanced by falling back on a more ancient state of things; we have reformed by calling to life again the institutions of earlier and ruder times, by setting ourselves free from the slavish subtleties of Norman lawyers, by casting aside as an accursed thing the innovations of Tudor tyranny and Stuart usurpation."

Again :—

" Our English constitution was never made in the sense in which the constitutions of many other countries have been made. There never was any moment when Englishmen drew out their political system in the shape of a formal document, whether as

[1] *See* "Growth of the English Constitution," by Freeman, pp. 20, 21. Macmillan, 1872.

the carrying out of any abstract political theories, or as the imitation of the past or present system of any other nation.

Till the Charter was wrung from King John, men called for the laws of good King Edward. We have made changes from time to time, but they have been changes at once conservative and progressive. They have been the application of ancient principles to new circumstances; they have been the careful repairs of an ancient building, not the pulling down of an old building, and the rearing up of a new.

Our national assembly has changed its name and its constitution, but its corporate identity has lived on unbroken. In France, on the other hand, institutions have been the work of abstract theory; they have been the creations for good or for evil of the minds of individual men." (Pp. 55, 64.)

And again :—

"There is, indeed, a wide difference between the political condition of England under Edward I. and the political condition of England in our own day, but the difference lies far more in the practical working of the constitution than in its outward form.

The changes have been many, but a large portion of those changes have not been formal enactments, but those silent changes whose gradual working has wrought out for us a conventional constitution existing alongside of our written law.

Speaking generally, and allowing for the important class of conventional understandings which have never been clothed with the form of written enactments, the main elements of the English constitution remain now as they were fixed then." (Pp. 86, 87.)

And again :—

"At last came the sixteenth century, the time of trial for many parliamentary institutions in many countries of Europe. Not a few assemblies which had once been as free as our own Parliament were, during that age, swept away or reduced to empty ormalities.

Then it was that Charles V. and Philip II. overthrew the free constitutions of Castile and Aragon; then it was that the States-General of France met for the last time but one before their last meeting of all, on the eve of the great Revolution.

In England parliamentary institutions were not swept away, nor did Parliament sink into an empty form; but for a while our parliaments, like all our other institutions, became perverted into instruments of tyranny."

Every act which has restrained the arbitrary prerogative of the Crown, every act which has secured or increased either the powers of Parliament or the liberty of the subject, has been a return, sometimes to the letter, at all times to the spirit of our earliest law." (Pp. 98, 137.)

These examples may suffice for Protestant nations. From the sixteenth century the interior government of all the Catholic States has been bad, but on the whole the masses of the people have remained faithful to the order, discipline, and established authority of the Church. Preserved for 200 years from the dangers of the Reformation, they were at length carried away by the great revolutionary movement of 1789, which was itself but the logical development of Protestantism.

Poland forms an exception, but we must not forget that she was coveted by two powerful potentates in the East and West, and that the exclamation of one of her magnates, "*Malo periculosam libertatem quam otiosum servitium,*" was a cry of self-defence against her powerful enemies, who at last succeeded in their guilty and oft-renewed attempts. In the present century there is but one Protestant country that has resisted all the revolutionary aspirations of 1789, and that country is England, whose inhabitants have remained Christian, and whose government alone since the Cæsarism of the Renaissance has preserved the forms of the ancient Catholic governments of the Middle Ages.

Unquestionably she merits much praise, and Catholics owe her a debt of gratitude on this matter; for them England has remained a model and a consolation: a model, because she is the representative of ancient historical and Catholic institutions; a consolation, because they can point to her as a specimen of what all European countries would have been but for the excesses of the Renaissance, the bigotry of the sectarians in the sixteenth century, the insolence of the governments of Louis XIV., the Regency, and Louis XV., the corruption of the encyclopædists, the revolutionary theories of the eighteenth century, and the liberal ideas of the nineteenth century—none of which arose from Catholicism.

Let us examine the present condition of South America, Spain, and France, for Italy (although a Catholic nation) is considered by our opponents to have entered their new path of salvation.

In South America many States that had been governed by European Powers during the eighteenth century found themselves suddenly cut adrift from them, and for the space of forty years had to struggle in the throes of anarchy.

These States were Mexico, Venezuela, and the Argentine Republic, all of which were governed by revolutionists or men who had adopted the principles of 1789.

We do not make special reference to Spain, because what we say of France is equally applicable to the country of the Cid. Only an unparalleled boldness or a profound contempt for the public can enable anyone to lay down the theory that the frequent revolutions in France are attributable to the Catholic Church.

The French as a body have doubtless remained steadfast in the faith of St. Remi, but we cannot pretend to find in this fact a solution to the question.

Freedom of worship is one thing, and liberty of conscience is another, but modern liberalism confuses them. Catholics admit of the former as a necessity of modern society.

There is no Catholic country in Europe where non-Catholic forms of worship have not been tolerated; and in countries where non-Catholics have formed an important part of the population, Catholic governments have never shrunk from granting toleration of worship. Cardinal Richelieu induced his master to sign the Edict of Nantes long before any Protestant State had granted any kind of toleration to Catholics. When Englishmen inveigh against Louis XIV.'s unfortunate revocation of that Edict, they seem to forget that at that very time the laws of England were inflicting the penalty of death upon any Catholic priest who ventured to offer the sacrifice of the Mass within that realm. The gratitude of Christendom has ratified the praise of the heroic deeds of Frenchmen, deeds which the historians of the Middle Ages had lauded in the proverb *gesta Dei per Francos*, comprehending in this last word, not only the actual French people, but the Franks of ancient Lorraine and the tribes settled along the borders of the right bank of the Rhine as far as Friesland.

It must not be forgotten that the country of St. Vincent de Paul has also given birth to Voltaire, and that the Little Sisters of the Poor are less honoured by literary men than Madame Georges Sand. Above all, we must carefully distinguish the extraordinary pressure to which official France has been subjected since the period of the Renaissance.

Without going as far back as Philippe-le-Bel, who professed the same doctrines as Herr Falck, and as John of Meung, the author of the second part of the "Roman de la Rose," it may be fairly asserted that since the period of the Reformation, France has never possessed a government strictly faithful to the doctrines of ecclesiastical civil law as taught by the Universal Church.

In order not to complicate what is simple in itself, let us ascertain what government France has possessed in the present century that could be designated as clerical. The governments of the restoration under Louis XVIII. and Charles X., though on the whole favourable to Catholicism, thought more of their own interests than of the glorification of the Church.

Nevertheless, previous to Marshal MacMahon they may be considered as the best that France has recently possessed, and many of the misfortunes of that country might have been avoided, and her monarchical constitution perfected and developed, if the basis of the ancient traditions and moral interests of the country had been consulted. From the time of Louis XVI. up to the present day, every government in France has been more or less hostile or indifferent to Catholic interests.

The civil constitution of the clergy, *the organic articles* of the Concordat, the imprisonment of Pope Pius VI., the capture of Pius VII., the evils that afflicted the pontificate of Pius IX., have all been directly or indirectly the work of the French authorities; the July government of Louis Philippe was liberal, that of Napoleon III. was the sponsor of Cavour and the accomplice of Bismarck, and the two Republics of 1848 and 1870 led to the assassination of two archbishops (Mgr. Affré and Mgr. Darboy), and numbers of the clergy.

To what political section of Frenchmen must we attribute the execution of Louis XVI., the proscription of the clergy who refused to sign the oath of allegiance to the convention, the institution of the National Guard, the citation of the Comte de Montalembert and Père Lacordaire before the court of peers, and the massacre of the hostages?

M. de Tocqueville has summed up the events that took place towards the close of the eighteenth century in the following sentence: "We were making steady progress when the Revolution came upon us."

Notwithstanding the recent terrible experiences of our century, France of the present day may be considered as advancing steadily, and this to such an extent that her enemies cannot for a moment ignore her existence.

French civilization is so powerful that even her conquerors feel the hand of her irresistible influence, according to the words of Horace, *Græcia capta ferum victorem cepit.*

The propagation of Protestant ideas was in a great measure due to official France, and the question might be asked, firstly, what would have become of Protestantism and Mahometanism if the government of France, instead of becoming their accomplice and abettor at critical periods of their history, had joined religiously with the Emperor of Germany to oppose them? and, secondly, what would have been the fate of the Electorate of Brandenbourg without the aid of France at the most critical period of its existence?

According to the theories of the deductive school those nations who are corrupted by the Catholic Church are condemned to a condition of political absolutism, moral slavery, and incurable poverty; although Italy and Belgium are allowed to be more prosperous than France or Spain, and more or less exceptions to the rule.

Many persons, however, question the fact that liberty is definitely established in those two countries, and in any case it is necessary for us to ascertain in what sense the word "liberty" is used.

An article in "*Il Diritto*" called *Italia nera* partially discloses it to us.

In this article the following sentence occurs: "I popoli di religione papale o sono gia morti o vanno morendi." "Those nations who profess the papal religion are either dead or dying."

The article proceeds to prophesy that all will be smooth in Italy as long as the Catholics do not avail themselves of the political liberty common to all, but that the day on which these wretched people begin to profit by the principles of the constitution, the incompatibility that exists between modern civilization and the ideas of the court of Rome will be apparent.

The uninitiated reader may well ask himself what this enlightened writer wishes to prove?

Whilst declaring that those nations that practise the religion of the Pope are dead or dying, he proceeds to state that a large number of these persons exist in Italy, and may probably become a power in the land.

That which may happen at some future day in the Italian peninsula is precisely what has happened in Belgium since the year 1840.

The public in general do not imagine that the Belgian Catholics are either dead or dying; on the contrary, there is much vitality and energy amongst them, they make a serious and practical use of the representative system, and firmly stand their ground against the shocks to which the modern system of liberty subjects them; and they are certainly no poorer in mind or material possessions than the liberals or Protestants, either in the past or present.

M. de Laveleye in the year 1875 wrote as follows:—

" One of the authors of the Belgian constitution, perhaps the most distinguished amongst them, said to me lately, with heartfelt sorrow, 'We believed that all that was necessary to found liberty was to proclaim it by separating Church and State. I begin to think that we deceived ourselves. The Church, relying on the country districts, seeks to impose her absolute power. The great cities, which have given in their adhesion to modern ideas, will not let themselves be enslaved without attempting resistance. We are tending like France towards civil war; we are already in a revolutionary position. The future appears big with troubles.' The elections of 1874 have begun to bring the danger to light. The elections for the Chambers have strengthened the clerical party, while those for the Communes have given power to the liberals in all the large towns.

Antagonism between the towns and the provinces, which is one of the causes of civil war in France, begins already to show itself in Belgium. As long as the government remains in the hands of prudent men, who are more disposed to serve their country than to obey the bishops, grave disorders need not be apprehended. But if the fanatics who openly accept the 'Syllabus' as their political programme, should attain to power, terrible shocks would follow."

Quinet, in his "History of the Revolution," says there are only two methods of solving religious questions, "one by the use of restraint, the other by perfect liberty," and then proceeds to demonstrate that the latter is practically useless, and restraint is necessary.

"If Luther and Calvin," he continues, "had been content with the mere establishment of liberty of worship without enforcing their dogmas, there would never have been the shadow of a religious revolution in the sixteenth century."

The same writer, in a letter addressed to Eugène Sue upon the religious and moral condition of Europe, openly declared that nothing but force had been successful for the destruction of an ancient belief.

We find in an article in the "*Revue de Belgique*" (Oct. 15th 1875), by M. Pergameni, a Belgian writer of the liberal school, under the title of "The Basis of Political Liberty," an apology for these antichristian doctrines, which though coarse in expression is perfectly clear and distinct.

The author, following the steps of M. Quinet, Eugène Sue, and an eccentric Englishman named Stephen, controverts the opinions of the liberal doctrinaires of the Manchester school, the unionists, and the Belgian constitution.

He treats political liberty as inefficacious, superannuated, and a thing of the past.

He considers it an imposition that liberty should be allowed to opponents.

"Liberty," he says, with the calmest assurance, "is a practical idea, a result of race, climate, and civilization."

The author deserves to be ranked amongst the number of unwilling apologists, for he goes on to say:—

"If men were governed here below by an infallible and superior law, if in some part of the heavens the Book of Truth was disclosed to us; if we could read without difficulty that which is consonant with, and that which is contrary to the ideal of society, the problem of truth would be quickly and easily solved.

Everything in conformity with this ideal would be lawful and permissible; everything opposed to it would be forbidden.

But, alas! such is not the case. Neglected children as we are, we have above us no infallible master to take us by the hand, and tell us what is truth.

Truth is, in fact, but our own creation; social necessities are what we define them to be.

Might alone creates, preserves, and fixes social necessities and rules of right, for right without might is only an expression.

In spite of what anyone may say to the contrary, not only is might superior to right, which does not signify much; but might actually is right."

A little further on M. Pergameni repeats the proposition as laid down by Stephen:—

"The question as to liberty being desirable or not, is as illogical as the question whether fire is good or bad."

There is doubtless a certain amount of truth in this premise, and no Catholics dispute it, but from the mouth or pen of one who repudiates all objective authority in this world, such a declaration of principle is suicidal.

M. Pergameni continues in the following strain:—

"Let us not lose time in endeavouring to convince our adversaries; the experience of centuries can alone decide who possesses truth, and which of us approaches the nearest to the social ideal.

We believe we are right, which is sufficient for us; and thenceforth our duty is to try and spread those ideas which we consider just, without troubling ourselves about liberty.

Furthermore, this tendency to put aside liberty as an auxiliary in the social strife becomes every day more manifest, in proportion as conservative opinion transforms itself, and gathers round the Catholic Church the oldest and most solid religious structure that men have raised.

Germany, Switzerland, and Italy have given us an example; let us follow in their steps.

In countries like England and the United States these questions are far more simple, and the liberty of association and worship is almost without limit.

But premonitory symptoms of agitation are already beginning to trouble this surface, apparently so calm; and the moment is rapidly approaching when these countries will find themselves face to face with the formidable problem of religious liberty.

They will act, we doubt not, with all the practical good sense of the Anglo-Saxon race, and will not lose their time in discussing whether certain measures of self-defence, such as the suppression of religious orders, is a blow to the liberty of the subject. Necessity makes the law and *salus populi suprema lex* are old axioms that mankind will never repudiate.

In Belgium, as in France, the situation is much more critical. We are in the midst of the fray; and Ultramontanism labours with alarming zeal in its work of absorption.

What should be our line of action? It is not sufficient to look on, and sing the praises of liberty, but we must rise up manfully, and seek to muzzle the Roman wolf.

Will it suffice, as many people imagine, to deprive the Church of her privileges, and to put literally into execution the formula of ' a free Church in a free State?'

We have a firm conviction that such a course would prove fatal, and be the cause of our destruction.

If the Belgian liberals wish to save their country and their idea, they will be obliged to resort to more energetic measures: they will have to work without ceasing for the suppression of convents and religious orders; they will have to wrest education from the hands of the clergy, and forcibly stop the extraordinary growth of miracles and pilgrimages, which are objects of shame and scandal to the country.

What are these measures to be?

There is no question as to the making of martyrs. The days are passed in which burning and torture can be inflicted for political opinions; the customs of society have altered, and people of this nineteenth century no longer possess the iron hearts of their forefathers; but although repression may have lost its aspect of ferocity, it nevertheless exists, for it is the sanction of right.

Fines, banishments, and imprisonments are perfectly lawful and justifiable, and there is no reason why such methods should not be employed.

Liberty, tolerance, free discussion, and mild ridicule will not gain for us, who are freethinkers and disciples of Voltaire, an iota in this struggle. On the contrary, the more we talk of liberty, and the more we amuse ourselves by turning miracles into ridicule, the more will superstition spread amongst the people. A fortress of granite, like the clerical system, cannot be overthrown by such mild measures.

If we wish to accomplish a serious work, we must ignore the doctrines of the constitution of 1830, and set aside our first bright dreams of liberty.

No one would deny that liberty may be sometimes excellent, but social life is a far greater treasure; and in order to preserve this latter, we must know how to make use of force.

Each act of our legislation is an example of this, for each encroaches upon the domain of liberty; and if we still further restrict this domain whenever it fetters our social ideal, we shall be acting logically, as men ought to act.

The principles by which we ought to be guided in this struggle are those of lawful self-defence and social preservation;

they are also those of human solidarity, a fact too much forgotten by the liberals of all countries.

It is high time that the men of progress should earnestly take up the question of the poorer classes, the number of which increases every day in so threatening a manner.

In this matter the clericals long ago took the wind out of our sails, and became the advisers, the rulers, and the comforters of the people.

Let us do as they have done—let us go to the disinherited, protect them against the machinations of the Church, if necessary even at the cost of liberty of association.

Let us bear in mind that the great law of all human societies is the struggle of opposite powers, that a political party can only retain its existence by active warfare; that it cannot afford to fall into a sleepy indifference, or to leave the ground to its adversaries; and that the true motto of every man who believes in an idea, is that of one of our champions of liberalism, De Marnix de Sainte Aldegonde, ' Rest is elsewhere.' "

Under this spirited passage of M. Pergameni there exists undoubtedly a certain sincerity of conviction; he says nothing stronger than many men of his school have done, though he may have expressed his opinions with greater clearness, but M. de Laveleye in the name of the committee of the "*Revue de Belgique*," thought it necessary to write the following disclaimer :—

"The system defended by M. Pergameni is accepted by none of the members of the committee. It has numerous partisans in England, Italy, France, and Germany (especially the latter), and their number will probably increase in proportion as the excessive pretensions of the clergy provoke an increased opposition."

Quinet, in a letter to Eugène Sue, acknowledges that it was difficult to formulate his doctrine, and that he therefore found it desirable to put it forward in a diluted manner. We conclude M. de Laveleye is of a similar opinion.

That the sentiments of M. Pergameni are not actually endorsed by all the members of the modern Continental school of liberalism is evident, for a large number take their stand from the historical point of view of our doctrinary and parliamentary liberals, and protest against them; but as a matter, nevertheless, of fact they are put into practice in Prussia and in Switzerland, two countries that profess to take the lead in modern civilization.

Prince Bismarck, who puts them in practice, is hailed as one of the greatest men of the day; and the ablest jurists, the most renowned men of letters, and those philosophers that Germany still possesses, bow down before him.

He wished to rebuke the overreaching of the Church, and he has ended by imprisoning or driving into exile almost all the Bishops in Prussia.

He was shocked at the interference of the Church

with human liberty, an interference suggested by the supernatural law, and he accordingly invented State laws which should put the "supernatural" beneath the feet of his soldiers and lawyers.

Under the pretext of acting on the defensive, a form of despotic tyranny was introduced. Such conduct never can stop on the defensive, it invariably proceeds to the aggressive, and finally develops into despotism.

Some of the modern school of liberals are more technical but less convincing; they seek to redress mistakes upon the notions of liberty, and put forward paternally philosophical admonitions.

We will not allow ourselves to be carried away by a digression which would inevitably ensue if we were to begin criticizing such theories. Doctrines of civil and political liberty, deduced exclusively from the notion of moral liberty, cannot be accepted without philosophical reserve, and would give rise to many rational objections. It is possible to entertain with regard to moral liberty the most approved philosophical doctrine without admitting liberty of worship as an absolute principle, and yet be a perfectly honest man; and it is possible in the same way to define liberty of worship doctrinally as a pestilence, and yet to respect with sincerity in its civil aspect a legislation which tolerates every form of worship.

Such is the argument and hypothesis of Catholics.

Many philosophers, we are aware, refuse to admit "absolute liberty of worship," and declare that it is only sophists who venture to maintain the possibility of such a thing as "absolute liberty."

"Liberty," they say, "cannot exist absolutely for mankind, since the liberty of each member of society is limited by the liberty of all the others.

Liberty has its limits, but that does not hinder it from being a thing desirable to acquire.

It is a thing that is good, because it is a thing that is right."

This argument is fundamentally fallacious: it confounds moral and political liberty and what is positive with what is relative, and entirely subverts the notion of good. Liberty is not a good thing because it is right; on the contrary, it can only become a right for the realization of good.

Who is to define the limits of civil liberty, when different writers set up different claims to do so, each in a different manner?

In what way can the encyclicals *Mirari vos* and *Quanta cura*, be called even "philosophically" inferior to the uncertain and subjective theories of the modern liberals?

In conclusion, Catholic nations are either dead or dying, but if perchance they have not yet been buried and become a thing of the past, governments must be cautious as to granting them any political liberties, which are only lawful for Protestants and liberals; and experience proves, and will prove every day more conclusively, that free thought cannot hold ground against Catholicism in the domain of absolute and complete liberty.

For this reason people are beginning to seek, contrary to the whole history of the past and the existing facts of the present, to prove that Catholics are religiously corrupt in soul, slaves in politics, and condemned by the laws of economy to a state of poverty.

When it is shown, as in Belgium, that such an argument is radically false and utterly untenable, they cry out that Catholics should be excluded from participating in the benefits of civil liberty and common law.

On the one hand, therefore, the assertion is made that Catholics are incapable of life; on the other, that they should be condemned to death because they have too much life.

If civil liberties ought not to be granted to Catholics as well as to other persons, what is the system proposed to be applied to them?

Persecution and tyranny, to be exercised according as the various governments of the day shall think advisable.

To such a pitch of "civilization and progress" have we arrived in the latter half of the nineteenth century.

CHAPTER VI.

CATHOLIC COUNTRIES AND EDUCATION.

Instruction in itself not a source of material prosperity—False conclusions as to the condition of public teaching in a country in regard to political power—Primary teaching in Belgium—In Prussia—The organization of primary instruction and the Reformation.

AFTER an endeavour to prove that the Reformation is more favourable than Catholicism to the development of nations, M. de Laveleye sets himself the task of finding out the causes of this imaginary fact. The first cause is supposed to be instruction, which in his opinion is more complete in Protestant than Catholic countries; by instruction he means the small amount of knowledge, both scientific and literary, that can be carried away from the elementary school.

Saxony, Denmark, and Sweden are said to occupy the first rank among nations, with populations almost entirely free from uneducated men, whilst France, Belgium, Spain, and Portugal stagnate in invincible ignorance.

Invincible ignorance, for though Catholic States may decree compulsory education, as Italy has done recently, or spend large sums for this purpose, like Belgium, they do not succeed in uprooting ignorance.

In England, where primary education is a little more complete than in Portugal, the apparent regularity of this syllogism is perverted, probably because the Anglican Church is amongst the Reformed Churches that which is most akin to the Church of Rome.

Holland might have been mentioned by the side of Great Britain.

In Switzerland we are told that the Latin but Protestant cantons of Neufchâtel, of Vaud, and of Geneva, are under this head on a par with the Teutonic cantons of Zurich and Berne, and superior to those of Ticino, Valais, and Lucerne.

The general cause of this extraordinary contrast is contained in the saying of Luther, "instruct the children." Protestants must all know how to read, since the reformed creed reposes upon a book, the

Catholic Countries and Education. 183

Bible, whilst with Catholics reading is the path that leads to heresy—in a word, the organization of primary instruction dates from the era of the Reformation.

Instruction being very favourable to the practice of political liberty, and to the production of riches, and Protestantism favouring as it does the diffusion of instruction, a manifest superiority is to be seen in Protestant States.

This chain of reasoning is contrary not only to reality, but even to the economical thesis of the writer, " Man does not live by bread alone, but by every word that proceedeth forth from the mouth of God."

Everyone is aware that riches, in the ordinary acceptation of the term, are not the general portion of the learned and well informed.

Stultitiam patiuntur opes.

It is not riches, nor even science, but justice that educates nations.

Justitia elevat gentes.

In the most refined period of the republic at Athens, none of the electors contemporary with Aristophanes were able to read or write.

Primary education did not make the fortune of either Tyre or Carthage.

When ancient Rome governed the earth with her

political dictatorship, the fellow-countrymen of Ovid, of Horace, and of Virgil, were not all normalists. In the present day England is recognized as one of the first political societies of the modern world, and yet she is one of the lowest in the scale of primary instruction. Russia, the actual umpire of European peace, is in this matter the most behindhand of all.

The consul who reduced the country of Plato and Pindar into a Roman province was an uneducated boor. Many unlettered men could be numbered amongst those who carried the banner of the immortal principles of '89 through Europe.

The schoolmaster may have triumphed at Sedan, but who triumphed at Jena? Compulsory instruction existed in Prussia long before 1789, and it did not prevent that country from undergoing political humiliation from the retreat of Champagne, under the Prince of Coburg, until the year 1813.

From the reports of school statistics, the country which may be considered as most advanced with regard to elementary education is Sweden, whose civilized districts are more or less on a par with the provinces of Limburg, Luxembourg, and Namur, in Belgium.

In spite of the secular *Schulzwang* of Prussia, the

monarchy of Frederic II. is not so advanced as the province of Arlon in Belgium.

The perfection of primary education is to be found in Luxembourg; the governor of that province in the opening session of the provincial council of the year 1872 spoke as follows :—

"Luxembourg counts at the present time 507 elementary schools—that is to say, one school to every 400 inhabitants; and such a result has not been attained in any other country in Europe.

It is the result of the united efforts of individuals, of districts, of provinces, and of the central power . . . . a wise and fruitful association.

The frequent and persevering attempts of Luxembourg to found schools is an interesting and touching history.

It was in itself a colossal undertaking, and local difficulties still further complicated it. The province has an exceptional territorial area ; it possesses no large centres, and its population is scattered in eight or nine hundred groups of villages. Most of the parishes are poor.

For the last fifty years the number of pupils in the elementary schools has been relatively large, and is perpetually on the increase.

In the year 1817 it was 10 per cent. of the population, and it now exceeds 15 per cent.

Last year the census proved that there were 31,580 children of an age to go to school, and the number of scholars actually attending the elementary schools was 31,239; so that only 341 children were missing, which produces 1 per cent.—a result that has never been attained in any country in Europe, under any educational system.

The entire population pass through the schools. For every 357 inhabitants there is one schoolmaster, whilst the proportion in the whole country is one to every 140 inhabitants.

In Brabant it is one to 507, and in the province of Liége one to 526.

We find the following in a parliamentary document recently published, and in which the condition of elementary education in the different parts of the world is thoroughly set forth and appreciated : 'The most praiseworthy part of the system in Switzerland, and that which best explains its success and its celebrity, lies undoubtedly in the great number of schools it possesses.'

In Switzerland there are not so many schoolmasters in proportion as in Luxembourg. Such superiority is not then merely local, and relative to the other Belgian provinces, it places Luxembourg above the countries the most favoured under this head.

Here, then, we have a picture of the organization of popular instruction produced by the happy dispositions of the population, of the law, and of time.

However the organization of the school is here a collection of means more or less well adapted, and the results of which are uncertain, according to times and places; the final end, the great duty, is the diffusion of instruction.

In what measure does this benefit extend to the population of Luxembourg? On this point, I often quote with curiosity the statistics, and all the elements of proofs that they can furnish.

In more than half of our districts ignorance is completely banished from the rising generation, as well amongst the women as amongst the men. In the remaining half it is, with the exception of some very backward localities, almost a thing of the past.

We may then truthfully assert that primary instruction in Luxembourg is almost universal."

In the provinces of Namur and Limburg, which are both Catholic, the same satisfactory results are obtained. Baron Kervyn de Lettenhove proved the other day in the Belgian Chamber of Representatives that his own district of Ecloo, which the liberals style "clerical," is far superior in its elementary instruction to the "liberal" town of Brussels, the capital of the kingdom.

It is well known to all who study such matters that the industrial districts of Liége, and of Mons in Belgium, which are the strongholds of liberal sentiments, are ranked amongst the most uneducated parts of the country.

The high degree of perfection attained by the Germans in their elementary system cannot be denied, but to attribute it to Lutheranism, or to the Prussian Union, would be a strange distortion of facts.

We are ready to admit, with certain reservations, that the *Schulzwang* (the civil obligation to frequent school) is productive of good, but the following important facts should not be forgotten:—(1) that the Swedish and German schools were until the year 1870 denominational; (2) that in Belgium, where Catholics enjoy liberty, elementary instruction is as far advanced as in Holland, and more advanced than it is in England; (3) that in Germany the Catholic districts are by no means inferior to those that are non-Catholic, and (4) that France can hold her own against the most prosperous and flourishing of the States in America.

As regards Switzerland, it is quite possible that in the cantons of the Valais and Ticino, and even in that of Lucerne, there should be less general primary instruction than in other cantons; but this fact, even if it be correct, is naturally explained by the difficulty of forming schools in mountainous districts inhabited by a scattered population.

Since the year 1870 it has become the fashion amongst a certain school to represent Prussia as the classical ground of every social and political truth, and to quote amongst these instruction in general, and elementary instruction in particular, as the special fruits of Protestantism. Now it will be found on investigation that the excellent system of education in Prussia is owing in a great measure to the Catholics.

A hundred years ago the margravate of Brandenbourg was with regard to elementary instruction one of the most backward States of Europe, and this after 200 years of Lutheran civilization.

During that period the Elector, to show his displeasure against some of the university professors, ordered them to be left naked on the ice.

The peasants were treated with the greatest severity, and the recruiting sergeant was much more respected than the few successors of the Catholic masters who had founded the ancient parochial and conventual schools. Elementary ignorance prevailed. Even in the reign of Frederic II., at the time when certain efforts had already been made towards changing a state of things so prejudicial to the population, no one thought of attaching to education the importance that has been given to it in the present day by Herr Falck and his admirers in foreign countries.

"The catechism and the four rules are sufficient" were the words (in a letter to Voltaire) of the philosopher Ring, who is now quoted as the precursor of national liberals.

In Silesia, which at that epoch formed part of the monarchy of the Hapsburgs, the situation was quite different. Every locality was provided with a school, either parochial or conventual.

In Lower and Middle Silesia there were many Protestants who enjoyed a satisfactory elementary education by reason of civil liberty, which did not then exist in the Protestant State of Brandenbourg, any more than at the present day.

When Frederic II. inaugurated the series of Prussian annexations by the forcible conquest of Silesia, he remembered the services rendered to his house by the Jesuits, in working for the transformation of the Duchy of Prussia into a kingdom.[1]

After the suppression of the society he maintained its members in many of the ancient colleges, which preserved their Catholic aspect though they were turned into State institutions.

Frederic II. protected the popular schools of the Augustinians, whose establishments eventually became model schools.

The prior of Sagan Felbiger and his famous *scholasticus*, Strauss, may be regarded as the real organizers of the old Prussian system, for the school regulations of 1801 were based on the institution of these clericals. In the new provinces of the West, similar facts are to be noticed. Quite recently a statue was erected at Munster in Westphalia in honour of Baron Furstenberg, who had brought popular instruction to the highest degree of prosperity.

---

[1] See "*Les Allemands depuis la guerre de sept ans*," by Baron de Haulleville. Brussels.

Catholic Countries and Education. 191

In this clerical scheme he had received the assistance of the well-known Overberg.

The establishment of schools throughout Prussia is due to Protestantism neither in the West nor in the East. The government inherited the original schools, which were Catholic, and the model of the present denominational institutions.

The present richness of popular instruction in Prussia is due to the scrupulous observance of their original character. Since 1870 the ruling powers seem to have become infatuated. The denominational aspect of elementary teaching has been radically suppressed, or at least perverted, and many persons believe that the superiority of the Prussian system is now doomed, since the life which the Catholic founders had breathed into it has been destroyed.

"No State," says M. Dahlmann, a celebrated Protestant Prussian of the old school, and professor of the University at Bonn, "has ever monopolized the education of children, to bring them up after its own fashion, without doing prejudice to the better part of the people; our foresight prevents us from selling souls to the State."

Protestants frequently assert that the organization

of popular instruction dates from the time of the Reformation, but this is incorrect.

Previous to the invention of typography, *i.e.* before the end of the fifteenth century, the Catholic clergy were the sole guardians of the wants of public instruction.

It is not within the scope of this work to enter into a description of the schools of the Middle Ages, from Charlemagne to Charles V., or to explain how the art of printing gave a new impetus to education, but the study is one of great interest and the subject but little known.

The enemies of the Catholic Church are inclined to confound her history with that of the Middle Ages, which should be kept totally distinct.

The schools of the Middle Ages did not equal those of our own day as regards their discoveries in science, chemistry, machinery, astronomy, and physics; but reading, writing, and the four rules of arithmetic were taught then exactly as they are now, and moral sciences (the most important of all) were taught in the professorial chairs of the universities with as much splendour as could be claimed for the most renowned modern academies of Germany.

Who amongst the German philosophers of the

Catholic Countries and Education.

present day can be compared to St. Thomas of Aquin, the great Dominican of the thirteenth century (the Angel of the Schools, as he was called), who taught and lectured in the various universities scattered throughout France, Germany, and Italy?

When illustrious writers like M. Donnet de Vorges and Dr. Van Weddingen see no hope for modern philosophy save in a deep study of ideology and scholastic metaphysics, we are filled with wonder, and contrast their language with that of those powerful minds who enlightened the world from the time of St. Bernard down to that of St. Ignatius of Loyola.

Albert the Great, Roger Bacon, the author of "The Imitation of Christ," Dante, and Petrarch are not inferior to Virchow, Haeckel, M. de Sybel, and Madame Louise Mühlbach; and few poems of modern times can be said to breathe forth the same depth of inspiration as the epic poems of the Middle Ages?

The statement is frequently made that Catholics are forbidden to read, as reading may lead to heresy, and that therefore they must be more ignorant than Protestants; and also that the Reformed Church rests upon a book.

In such an assertion two fallacies may be detected:

(1st), Catholics do read, and are not afraid of study—witness the names of such men as Bossuet, Fénelon, Massillon, Corneille, Racine, Balmez, Lingard, Dupanloup, Ketteler, Newman, Secchi, Waterton, Manning, Paley, Hergenröther, Wiseman, &c. &c.; (2nd), Protestant Churches do not rest upon the Bible, but upon the symbolical Scriptures.

Luther certainly professed to teach the doctrine of the private interpretation of each individual, but for all that he did not admit that anyone should resist his interpretation. He took good care to lose no time in drawing up with the aid of his friends and partisans a creed called "The Confession of Augsburg," which the princes enriched with the spoils of the Church disseminated throughout their districts by the help of fire and sword.

This new creed cannot properly be called biblical, since the doctrines it teaches upon grace and faith without works are not to be found in the pages of Holy Writ.

The diffusion of instruction has nothing in common with the Protestant doctrine of private interpretation, for Protestants scarcely ever apply this latter to their religious teaching, preferring the system of the Catholic Church (*auctoritative*).

It may be as well to add that Luther's efforts in favour of public instruction date only from the second part of his career.

The destruction of canonries, of convents, and of monasteries which Catholic piety had thickly planted throughout the land, brought in their train the ruin of the schools that were supported by the secular and regular clergy.

In a short space of time a frightful falling off ensued, both in instruction and morals, and it was at this critical period of his existence that Luther found his work was threatened, and began to expatiate unceasingly upon the necessity of public education.[1]

Luther's doctrine on grace and on the real presence gave rise, as is well known, to the most lively disputes between his partisans and those of Calvin and Zwingle respectively. Each party laid claim to a doctrinal infallibility demonstrated by Scripture, and these opposite pretensions were more than once defended, not by means of briefs and encyclicals, but by the sword, and the material victory of the one entailed as a consequence the moral oppression of the other.

"The Confession of Augsburg" was opposed in

[1] *See* Works of Luther, Walsche, Menzel.

the West of Germany by the Reformed Church proper.

The rulers of the different Protestant States of the old Germanic Empire adopted either "The Confession of Augsburg," or "The Catechism of Heidelberg," according as such a change suited their fancy or their temporal interests.

The people who theoretically possessed the right of private interpretation were not consulted, any more than the clergy, and yet both were entitled to have an opinion on the subject as well as their rulers. The variations of official Prussia eclipse all the other German States, and "The Confession of Augsburg" is interesting, inasmuch as it gives great insight into its religious theories.

In consequence of an alliance with the House of Orange, the Dutch reformed worship became prevalent at the Court of Brandenbourg, and the Lutheran preachers were morally and sometimes even physically compelled to permit Calvinist doctrines to be propounded from their pulpits.

Calvinist pastors were quietly forced upon Lutheran parishes, and those Lutherans who refused to submit to this form of free interpretation were brutally deposed and banished in much the same fashion as

Catholic priests are treated in the present day under the ministry of Herr Falck.

We may cite Gerhard, well known throughout Europe for the services he rendered to the development of Protestant church music, as amongst the victims of the Calvinistic heresy.

The greater number of preachers preferred to preserve their posts by the adoption of "The Catechism of Heidelberg," and were obedient to the commands of the Court.

After the Congress of Vienna, in 1815, which, as is well known, gave to Prussia a new portion of territory inhabited by Lutheran Saxons, the official Church of Prussia, under the military pastoral staff of its chief bishop the king, ordered a fusion of the two creeds by means of an *Union* in the Sacrament, which Union was carried out with the greatest coolness and precision. On the 30th June, 1817, an order from the Minister of Home Affairs abolished the names of Lutheran and Calvinistic Churches, and also the historically significant and distinctive name of Protestant Church, and commanded the general use of the name Evangelical Church alone.

The Berlin Synod had framed this new Church to suit the king, and by an equivoque unworthy of

Christian men, or men sitting upon public affairs of religious import, framed the external observances so that any man might partake of the Lord's Supper in this new Church without being less a Lutheran or Calvinist than he was before.

Some few communities declared themselves free, whilst others found consolation in silently permitting a generous but barren form of pietism to be imposed upon them from high quarters.

Enlightened men adopted Hegel's doctrine of the State being the divine ruler in the place of God, but the mass of the people were insensibly converted to the Union by their schoolmasters and the aid of the military.

The Prussian Union has shown itself to be a veritable State Church, and may be said to be crumbling away before our eyes, since the rite of baptism is no longer legally requisite, and civil marriage has been introduced into the code of law.

The middle classes take little heed of the perilous position of their Church, a civilizing form of scepticism serves them as a provisional retrenchment under the protection of an army of 12,000 men.

The Prussian Union was an attempt to impose new shackles on the human mind, to turn religion into a support of despotism, and to train the Prussian mind as the Russian mind is trained, into a religious veneration for, and worship of the supreme autocratic head of the State.

The principle that the civil government or State is entitled to regulate the religious belief of a country has more of intellectual thraldom in it than the power of the Catholic Church could ever have exercised according to the belief of Protestants in the darkest ages, for it had no civil power joined to its religious power.

The Catholic Church was an independent, distinct, and often an opposing power in every country to the civil authority, a circumstance in the social economy of the Middle Ages to which Europe is indebted for her civilization and freedom.

When governments attempt to extend their power beyond the legitimate object for which government is established in society, and wish to embrace the intellectual, moral, and religious concerns as well as the material interests of their subjects, they are obliged to adopt a middle course between the extreme of power they would usurp and the innate principle in the human mind of resistance to power over intellectual action.

This middle course, founded on no principle but the evasion of applying principle to action, has been the line of policy of most European statesmen during this century.

Whilst Europe was singing the praises of the Prussian system of education, this same system was driving upwards of 600 Christians from the land by religious persecution, who went from Silesia to the wilds of America, in order that they might worship the Almighty after their own fashion rather than at the dictation of their sovereign.

Whilst the condition of Prussia as regards education stood undoubtedly high, her moral state was so low that a sect called the Muckers, who openly taught the most disgusting practices and observances,[1] embraced hundreds of the nobility and clergy.

If to read, write, and cipher be education, the Prussians are an educated people; but if to reason, judge, and act as an independent free agent in the religious, moral, and social relations of man to his Creator and to his fellow-men be that exercise of the mental powers which alone deserves the name of education, then are the Prussians utterly deficient.

[1] *See* Laing's "Notes of a Traveller."

The intellectual dependence of the people upon the government, the abject submission to the want of freedom, or free agency, in thoughts, words, or acts, the religious thraldom of the people to forms which they despise, the want of influence, of religious and social principle in society, justify us in our statements.

The working classes in the Protestant districts of Pomerania, Brandenbourg, Eastern and Western Prussia proper, Schleswig, Holstein, and Saxony are drifting by steady progress towards socialism, which is called "the religion of the future."

The present is a strange moment for the liberals to choose in order to proclaim the advantages to be derived from the reading of the Bible, when it is a known fact that few persons read it in the Protestant parts of Germany, especially since the *Protestantenverein* has disseminated the criticisms of Strauss against that holy book.

The present administration of Prussia has made efforts to restrict the reading of the Bible in the schools, and there are throughout Germany men who flourish on the heights of civilization who consider that the youth of our day are too intelligent to lose time over the reading of "legends" that command respect, but that cannot brook the light of modern science.

They reason like Schiller, in his famous lines:—

> "Welche Religion ich bekenne? Keine von allen
> Die du mir nennst. Und warum Keine?
> Aus Religion."[1]

Religious disorganization has attained such alarming proportions throughout the northern districts of Germany that Catholics are anxious to see no further decrease in the numbers of believing Protestants, for though they may not be members of the true Church, they yet have some belief in the truths of a revealed religion.

Before concluding this subject we will prove still further by the light of history the ignorance of those persons who accuse Catholics of favouring ignorance.

Without going as far back as the "dark ages," when according to the testimony of the Protestant historian Voigt, Pope Gregory VII. urged all the bishops to protect arts and letters, and to found schools[2] in connection with their cathedral churches, we will quote

---

[1] [Translation.] "You ask me what religion I profess? No one of these which you name. And wherefore no one of them? For religion," .... &c.

[2] *See* "Why are we Catholics?" by Keenan.

Catholic Countries and Education. 203

the opinions of Burke, of Gibbon, and of Hutchinson. The first declared that France alone had produced more remarkable men than all the Protestant universities of Europe; the second, that one monastery of Benedictine monks had produced more scientific books than all the universities of England; and the third expressed himself in Parliament to the effect that "Catholicism, which has been to-night the object of so many insults, was at one period the religion of the most numerous, the religion of the most enlightened nations of Europe, and the religion of the most famous characters who have ever honoured the name of man."[1]

The proverb that "Ignorance is the mother of vice," was a common saying in the Church long before the birth of Luther, but the great circumstance which has favoured the calumny of the adversaries of the Catholic Church exists in the fact that the invention of printing scarcely preceded by seventy years the introduction of Protestantism into Europe.

Before the end of the fifteenth century printing presses were founded in thirty-four towns of France, and from the year 1455 to 1536, 22,032,900 volumes were printed.

The Popes Nicholas V. and Sixtus IV. are cele-

[1] *See* Cobbett, Lingard.

brated in history for their protection of the sciences and arts, and for their munificence in the advancement of education.

Ten universities were founded in Germany between the years 1403 and 1506.

Since the Reformation (for the space of 300 years) Protestants have founded but two universities (London and Dublin). Modern Europe is indebted to the Catholic Church for its civilization, its laws, its knowledge of the fine arts, for the origin of painting, of sculpture, of music, and of architecture.

The magnificent abbeys and cathedrals that have escaped the Vandalism of the Reformation, and the ruins of those buildings which the ravages of Calvinists and Puritans have not altogether destroyed, are living witnesses of this fact.

"Religion and civilization can never repay the debt they owe to the pontiffs or the Church of Rome, who for so long a period made the most noble efforts to advance mankind upon the path of progress."[1]

The statement that Catholics are forbidden to read the Scriptures is scarcely worthy of refutation.

No one who has studied the literature of the Middle Ages can have failed to perceive the strongest evidence

[1] "Life of Wallenstein," by Colonel Mitchell.

Catholic Countries and Education.

of the deep biblical knowledge it contains. Maitland,[1] in his "Dark Ages," writes thus:—

"The writings of the dark ages are made of the Scriptures. I do not merely mean that the writers constantly quoted the Scriptures, and appealed to them as authorities on all occasions; but I mean that they thought and spoke and wrote the thoughts and words and phrases of the Bible, and that they did this constantly and habitually as the natural mode of expressing themselves."

Further on the same writer adds :—

"I cannot help suspecting that if Robertson had gone to the Archbishop of Seville in the seventh century, the Archbishop of Mayence in the ninth, or the Bishop of Chartres in the eleventh, for holy orders, he would have found the examination rather more than he expected." P. 25.

Again he says :—

"A monk was expected to know the Psalter by heart." P. 338.

Further on he quotes the famous example of the sermon of the Bishop of Noyon in the seventh century, which Robertson and Mosheim quote as evidence of the barren theology of that age, and remarks :—

"It seems to have been written as if the author had anticipated each and all of Mosheim's charges, and intended to furnish a pointed answer to every one." P. 113.

"In the eighth and ninth centuries," says Hallam

[1] "The Dark Ages," by the Rev. S. R. Maitland, librarian to the Archbishop of Canterbury. P. 470.

("Middle Ages," iii. 474), "when the Vulgate had ceased to be generally intelligible, ... translations were freely made into the vernacular languages."

We quote a passage from a work entitled "The Reading of the Bible in the Vulgar Tongue," from the pen of Monsignor Malou, Bishop of Bruges :—

> "Has the Church made any law forbidding her children the reading of the Holy Scriptures? I do not hesitate to answer, No. The Church has never forbidden to the faithful the reading of the Bible in any language whatsoever, nor has she authorized any monopoly in favour of the clergy."

The Church has certainly decreed wise restrictions, acting according to the words of St. Peter, who said that certain portions of the epistles of St. Paul "are difficult, hard to be understood, which the unlearned and unstable wrest to their own destruction."[1]

The prohibition explains itself.

The rule approved of by Benedict XIV. in 1757, which granted to all the faithful the general permission to read the Scriptures in the vulgar tongue, provided the version had received the approval of competent authority, is a decree of the Congregation of the Index.

The Church causes portions of the Scriptures to be read to the assembled faithful in her daily offices.

---

[1] *See* Second Epistle of St. Peter, chap. iii. verse 16.

In the year 1826 the English Catholic Bishops publicly declared that the Church had never prevented the circulation of authentic copies of Holy Writ.[1]

Pius VII., in a letter addressed to the same, dated 18th of April, 1826, made use of the following injunction:—

"To exhort the faithful to read the Sacred Scriptures, since nothing is more beneficial and more calculated to console and comfort them."

Pius VI., writing to Martini, Archbishop of Florence, on the subject of his translation of the Bible, congratulates him on his zeal in publishing it, and exhorts the faithful to study it. The letter is dated April, 1778, and may be found in the title-page of most Catholic versions of the Sacred Scriptures.

Before the birth of Protestantism, upwards of twenty translations of the Bible in the principal modern languages existed.

The following is an enumeration of some of these old translations:—

Bible of Just, at Mayence, in	. . . .	1462
,, Bender, at Augsburg, in	. . .	1467
,, Malermi, in Italy, in	. . . .	1471

[1] A pamphlet has recently been published by the Rev. Kenelm Vaughan, entitled "The Popular Use of the Bible Encouraged by the Catholic Church."

The four Gospels in Flemish, in	1472
The entire Bible in Low Dutch, in	1475
Bible of Julien, in	1477
,, Delft, in	1477
,, Ferrier, in Spanish, in	1478
,, Gouda, in	1479
,, Des Moulins, in French, in	1490
Four translations mentioned by Beausobre ("Histoire de la Reformation," book iv.), printed before	1522

To this enumeration must be added the following list of manuscripts:—

Bible in English, in	1290
,, Anglo-Saxon, in	1300
,, German, in	800
,, Italian, in	1270
,, Spanish, in	1280
,, French, in	1294

Previous to Luther there were three translations and many editions of the Bible published in Italy, four translations and a vast number of editions in Gothic and in French, and two translations and several editions in Flemish.

A Czech translation was published in Prague, in the year 1488, at Putna in 1498, and at Venice in 1506 and 1511.

A large number of translations in almost every language of the world were published in Rome.

Catholic Countries and Education.

The prejudices of many people are, however, so deeply seated against everything Catholic, that it is a work of some difficulty to persuade them that Luther was not the first translator of the Bible into German.

Before his lamentable apostacy, there were twenty-one German translations extant (fifteen in High German and six in Low German). Luther himself made use of the translation of Nicholas of Lyra (which appeared in 1473, and went through several editions before the Reformation), and to such an extent that a facetious poet clothed the well-known fact in these words, "*Si Lyra non lyrasset, Lutherus non saltasset.*"

A Presbyterian writer,[1] in his "Notes of a Traveller," makes the following admissions:—

"The education of the clergy of the Catholic Church is positively higher and, beyond doubt, comparatively higher than the education of the Scotch clergy.

By positively higher is meant that among a given number of Popish and of Scotch clergy a greater proportion of the former will be found who read with ease, and a perfect mastery, the ancient languages of Greek and Latin, and the Hebrew and the Eastern languages connected with that of the Old Testament—a greater number of profound scholars, a greater number of high

---

[1] *See* "Notes of a Traveller," by Laing. Longmans, London, 1842.

mathematicians, and a higher average amount of acquired knowledge.

It is very much owing to the zeal and assiduity of the priesthood in diffusing instruction in the useful branches of knowledge, that the revival and spread of Catholicism have been so considerable among the people of the Continent, who were left by the Revolution, and the warfare attending it, in that state that if the Catholic religion had not connected itself with something visibly useful, with material interests, they would have had nothing to do with it.

The Catholic clergy adroitly seized on education—not as most of us suppose in Protestant countries, to keep the people in darkness and ignorance, and to inculcate error and superstition—but to be at the head of the great social influence of useful knowledge, and with the conviction that this knowledge (reading, writing, arithmetic, and all such acquirements) is no more thinking, or an education leading to thinking, and to shaking off the trammels of Popish superstition than playing the fiddle, or painting, or any other acquirement to which mind is applied."

With reference to the stupid assertion that the Catholic clergy leave the people in ignorance, he writes as follows :—

"This opinion of Protestants is more orthodox than charitable or correct. The Popish clergy have in reality less to lose by the progress of education than our own Scotch ministers, because their pastoral influence and their Church services being founded on ceremonial ordinances, come into no competition or comparison whatsoever in the public mind with anything similar that literature or education produces ; and are not connected with the imperfect mode of conveying instruction which, as education advances, becomes obsolete, and falls into disuse, and almost into contempt, although essential in our Scotch Church.

Catholic Countries and Education.

In Catholic Germany, in France, Italy, and even Spain, the education of the common people in reading, writing, arithmetic, music, manners, and morals is at least as generally diffused and as faithfully promoted by the clerical body as in Scotland.

It is by their own advance, and not by keeping back the advance of the people, that the Popish priesthood of the present day seek to keep ahead of the intellectual progress of the community in Catholic lands; and they might, perhaps, retort on the Protestant clergy, and ask if they, too, are in their countries at the head of the intellectual movement of the age?

Education is in reality not only not repressed, but is encouraged by the Popish Church, and is a mighty instrument in its hands, and ably used.

In every street in Rome, for instance, there are, at short distances, public primary schools for the education of the children of the lower and middle classes in the neighbourhood.

Rome, with a population of 158,678 souls, has 372 public primary schools, with 482 teachers, and 14,099 children attending them.

Has Edinburgh so many public schools for the instruction of those classes?

I doubt it. Berlin, with a population about double that of Rome, has only 264 schools.

Rome has also her university, with an average attendance of 660 students; and the Papal States, with a population of two and a half millions, contain seven universities.

Prussia, with a population of fourteen millions, has but seven.

These are amusing statistical facts, and instructive as well as amusing, when we remember the boasting carried on about the Prussian educational system for the people, and the establishment of governmental schools, and enforcing by police regulations the school attendance of the children of the lower classes.

The statistical fact that Rome has above a hundred schools

more than Berlin, for a population little more than half of that of Berlin, puts to flight a world of humbug about systems of national education carried on by governments, and their moral effects on society.

Is it asked what is taught to the people of Rome by all these schools? Precisely what is taught at Berlin—reading, writing, arithmetic, geography, history, languages, religious doctrine of some sort, and, above all, the habit of passive submission in the one city to the clerical, in the other to the government authorities.

The Continental people had a religion to choose at the beginning of this century. How have the two Churches of Europe availed themselves of this peculiar state of the European mind?

The Protestant Church is shaken to the foundation in her ancient seats in Germany and Switzerland; and as a body politic has lost, instead of gaining influence.

The Roman Catholic Church has held the bridle, has entered more fully into the spirit of the age, and has exerted its elasticity to cover with the mantle of Catholicism, opinions wide enough to have formed irreconcilable schisms and sects in former ages.

The Catholic religion adapts itself to every degree of intelligence, and to every class of intellect.

I strolled one Sunday evening in Prussia into the Roman Catholic church at Bonn. The priest was catechizing, examining, and instructing the children of the parish, in the same way, and upon the same plan, and with the same care to awaken the intellectual powers of each child by appropriate questions and explanations, as in our well-conducted Sunday schools.

And what of all subjects was the subject this Catholic priest was explaining and inculcating to Catholic children, and by his familiar questions, and their answers, bringing most admirably home to their intelligence?—the total uselessness and inefficacy of mere forms of prayer, if not understood and accompanied by mental occupation with the subject, and the preference of silent mental prayer to all forms; and this most beautifully brought out to suit the intelligence of the children."

The assertion that progress and Protestantism go hand in hand is as false as the assumption that doctrinal purity was begotten by the apostacy of Luther.

Evidence of the kind we have quoted, given by our opponents, ought to open the eyes of those most blinded by prejudice to the fact that the Catholic Church not only loves but encourages art and science.

The following are the words of the present Pontiff, Leo XIII., on this subject :—

"How grand and full of majesty does man appear when he arrests the thunderbolt, ... summons the electric flash, ... how powerful when he takes possession of the force of steam. .... Is there not in man when he does these things some spark of creative power? .... The Church views these things with joy."[1]

The Catholic Church respects science because it comes from God.

"Catholicism is the greatest and the holiest school of respect that the world has ever possessed."

Such are the words of M. Guizot,[2] and they are

[1] *See* Lenten Pastoral for 1877, by Cardinai Pecci, now Pope Leo XIII., entitled "The Church and Civilization." Published in English by McGlashan and Gill, 50, Upper Sackville Street, Dublin.

[2] *See* "*Méditations et Études morales*," by M. Guizot.

applicable to the Catholic Church, and to her alone, although many people have made the attempt to include the various Protestant sects under the term of Catholicism.

CHAPTER VII.

RELATIVE MORALITY OF CATHOLIC AND PROTESTANT COUNTRIES.

Literary corruption in France, the consequence of anti-Catholic doctrines—Political absolutism the antithesis of the Catholic Church—The Catholic Church the only authority that has maintained the positively moral character of marriage—Morals in Spain and Italy contrasted with those in Protestant countries—Average illegitimacy greater amongst the latter—Immorality in the north of Europe—Statistics of immorality in England.

THE assertion is frequently made by the modern school of liberals that all the continental literature that is in vogue is vitiated by a current of immorality, and that those nations which may be designated as Catholic are more immoral than those that are Protestant.

In order to appreciate things in their true light it is

necessary to bear in mind, with regard to the literature thus denounced, that the writers, although nominally Catholic by the accident of their birth, practically reject the teaching of the Church, and are therefore outside her pale. In almost every case they borrow their weapons of war from Paganism and the principles of the Renaissance. Thus most of the literary characters and politicians in France who have worked for the emancipation of the mind have been tainted with a shade of immorality, whilst those who respect morals are, in almost every instance, partisans of the Church.

In England and America men uphold at the same time synonymously religion, morality, and liberty.

M. Taine, a Positivist, and M. Prevost-Paradol make the assertion that the principle of morality in France is based on honour, whilst in England it is based on a sense of stern duty.

There is much that is true in these arguments, though there are many misconceptions. For instance, the principal writers in vogue in France, such as Sainte-Beuve, About, Sardou, and Alexandre Dumas, are all anti-Catholic in sentiment and feeling; their works are deeply tinged with immorality, but they have been translated into English and German, and form some of the most popular literature in England and Prussia.

The giants of contemporary French literature, such as Châteaubriand, Gratry, Autran, Laprade, Montalembert, Dupanloup, and Lacordaire, have all been Catholics; and it is a remarkable fact that some of the most eminent writers throughout Europe, such as Dr. Newman and Dr. Lingard in England, Joseph Görres in Germany, Manzoni in Italy, and Balmez in Spain have been also Catholics.

We do not wish to deny that the pious remnant of Protestants in the present day are more pure, more moral, and more Christian than Mirabeau (the friend of Frederick II.), Saint Just, and Robespierre, nor do we refuse to admit that sincere Protestantism (*i.e.* incomplete Christianity) is superior to Paganism; but no proof of moral superiority of Protestantism over the Universal Church ever has or ever will be shown.

Let it be clearly understood that we do not claim for Catholics impeccability from the mere fact that they accept the decrees of the Church. It is not sufficient to profess the faith; to be a real Catholic it is necessary to put its teaching into practice and fulfil its precepts.

It must also be borne in mind that in Catholic

countries such as Belgium, France, Italy, Spain and Portugal, and parts of Germany, social and political revolutions, fomented by *the social influence of Protestantism*, have produced a state of things that renders it very difficult, not to say impossible, to distinguish those that are real Catholics from the mass of the nominal Catholic population. Everywhere the good grain is found mingled in close proximity with the bad. One thing is certain, that, even from the historical point of view, no Church in the annals of the world has maintained with such force the Divine precepts of the Sixth[1] and Ninth Commandments as the Catholic Church. Numbers of people would be excellent Catholics if they could suppress these two obstacles that obstruct the indulgence of their passions.

The curse of the heresy of the sixteenth century

---

[1] The division of the Ten Commandments used by the Catholic Church is here followed. Amongst Protestants the allusion would refer to the seventh and tenth.

The Commandments as given in Holy Scripture are not divided at all. Hence it has come to pass that two different methods of dividing them have prevailed. Among the Jews that arrangement was followed which Protestants have adopted, and this distribution is to be found in some of the Fathers. But the arrangement used in the Catholic Church is that which was followed by St. Augustine, and upheld as the most natural.

consisted in the fact that it denied the sacramental character of marriage, and thus lowered the tone and standard of morality.

The Evangelical Consistory assembled in full council, authorized Philip, the generous Elector of Hesse, on the strength of Melancthon's tolerant maxims, to seat two Electresses upon the throne at the same time.

The King of Prussia, Frederick William II., who had given his right hand to his queen, gave his left to Countess Julia Von Voss.

This second marriage ceremony was performed on the 25th of May, 1787, in the chapel of the castle at Charlottenburg, by Zoellner, the chaplain of the royal family at the Court.

Liberalism, which is in some respects a degeneration from Protestantism, is doctrinally incapable of stemming the natural consequences of the suppression of the sacrament of marriage.

Outside the Catholic faith practised in spirit and in truth, people can doubtless be chaste, but it is because they more or less put in practice the teaching and habits of the Church.

In order to be able to make the assertion that the sincere practice of the Catholic faith can produce immorality, one must be totally ignorant of the whole organization of the Church, of the teaching it embodies, and the whole spiritual conditions of its existence. It is, in fact, a logical contradiction. Much has been said since the Franco-Prussian war of 1870 about the immorality of the French, which is supposed to have proved itself an ally to the schoolmaster at Sedan, and we are aware that the greatest military authority in the German army sung the praises of German morality, from which time may be dated the phrase so often made use of in the press, that Berlin is " the city of pious manners and customs, and of the fear of God."

It is true that in many parts of France, such as Paris and the departments around it, an immense amount of immorality prevails, but these departments are precisely those in which the influence of the Catholic Church is at its lowest ebb, and has been opposed with the greatest amount of success.

A cosmopolitan city like Paris cannot be rightly cited as a Catholic town, especially as since the period of the Revolution more than half of its population are in bitter opposition to the teaching of the Church, and it is the centre and focus of the worthless and frivolous of Europe.

In Berlin vice does not enjoy, as in Paris, a vogue

organized by literary characters, but without the refinement of the French, a gross form of bestiality is prevalent which cannot be exceeded in Europe.

In the year 1837 the number of females in the Prussian population between the beginning of their sixteenth year and the end of their forty-fifth year, was 2,983,146: the number of illegitimate children born in the same year was 39,501, so that one in every seventy-five of the whole of the females of an age to bear children, had been the mother of an illegitimate child.

Prince Pukler Muskau[1] states in one of his publications that the character of the Prussians for honesty stands far lower than that of any other of the German populations, and as a Prussian he would scarcely come to such a conclusion unless it were generally believed in Germany.

Laing says:—

"It is an undeniable fact that the Prussians are in a remarkably demoralized condition in those branches of moral conduct which cannot be taught in schools, and are not taught by the parents, because parental tuition is broken in upon by the interference of the government. Of all the virtues that which the domestic family education of both the sexes most obviously influences, that which marks more clearly than any other the

[1] "*Südöstlicher Bildersaal,*" 3 vols., 1844.

moral condition of a society, the home state of moral and religious principles, the efficiency of those principles in it, and the amount of that moral restraint upon passions and impulses which it is the object of education and knowledge to obtain, is undoubtedly female chastity.

And yet I think no traveller or no Prussian will say that this index-virtue of the moral condition of a people is not lower in Prussia than in almost any other part of Europe.

It is no uncommon event in the family of a respectable tradesman in Berlin to find upon his breakfast-table a little baby of which he has no doubt at all about the maternal grandfather.

Such accidents are only regarded as youthful indiscretions, and not as disgraces, affecting as with us the respectability and happiness of many a generation." [1]

All the social errors of France are to be found in Prussia, though possibly not so visibly apparent to the public.

To appreciate the horrors of French vice it is necessary to seek for it in the translations of French works that appear in London and Berlin, in which places divorce has attained proportions unheard of in the history of any Catholic people. Even admitting that Paris is the most demoralized of European cities, side by side with this debasement may be found the radiant sun of charity and good works, to a degree far in excess of any other city of similar size.

We may sum up in a few words the abyss which

[1] Laing's "Notes of a Traveller," p. 167.

separates the moral condition of Paris from that of London and Berlin by stating that in Paris the Sisters of Charity are honoured, and the Little Sisters of the Poor protected, whilst in London they are only beginning to be tolerated and in Berlin they are actually proscribed.

In a study upon public health and morality by Dr. Fonsagrives of Montpellier the following statements occur:—

"It is proved that there is in Europe an average illegitimacy of fifteen children upon every hundred births. I thought it would be an interesting study to compare the extent of legitimacy amongst the European nations of Teutonic and Latin origin, and I found that it was 15 per cent. with the former, and 6·11 per cent. with the latter."

The statistics recently published (1876) by the Committee of the high Evangelical Consistory on the relative proportion of legitimate to illegitimate births are as follows in the Evangelical parishes of the various districts:—

Hohenzollern	2·50 per cent.
Westphalia	2·65 ,,
Rhine Provinces	2·79 ,,
Posen	6·77 ,,
Prussian Saxony	9·12 ,,
Brandenbourg (except Berlin)	9·16 ,,
Prussia Proper	9·58 ,,

Pomerania	9·95 per cent.
Silesia	10·15 ,,
Berlin	12·91 ,,

The Evangelical Church of Prussia is thus shown by her own confession to be losing her moral and religious ascendency over the minds of the great mass of the population.

The amount of immorality in Sweden and Norway is prodigious.[1]

Bayard Taylor wrote in the year 1858 that the Church of Sweden appeared to be becoming petrified by pure inertia. Not a single literary production can be cited in the kingdom of Sweden calculated to advance the interests of religion or morality.

Laing, in his "Notes of a Traveller," from which we have already quoted, says :—

"Religion has less influence upon public morals than in any other Christian communion.

In the streets of Stockholm one out of every three persons is illegitimate, and out of forty-nine, one is at least guilty of criminal offences."

And yet Inglis, another Protestant traveller, is not afraid to assert that the degree of morality in Sweden is far higher than that in Norway.

In this latter country, indifference towards every

[1] *See* Marshall's "Christian Missions," vol. ii. p. 544.

kind of religion is prevalent. It is scarcely necessary to mention Denmark, the country that gave rise to the sect of the Mormons, and where, in the years 1777 and 1789 the pain of death was decreed against any Catholic priest who should place his foot upon Danish soil.

In Switzerland the discordance between the religious and material state of the people is extraordinary. Most travellers are struck with the contrast in the material condition of the Catholic and Protestant cantons, and also with the influence of religion over each. This influence is at its minimum in Protestant cantons and at its maximum in those that are Catholic.

Laing writes as follows :—

"Geneva, the seat and centre of Calvinism, the earthly source, the pattern of our Presbyterian doctrine and practice, has fallen lower from her own original religion and practice than ever Rome fell.

Rome has still superstition, Geneva has not even the semblance of religion. In the head-church of the original seat of Calvinism, in a city of 25,000 souls, at the only service on the Sabbath day, I sat down in a congregation of two hundred females and twenty-three males, mostly elderly men of a former generation.

In no country in Europe is church attendance worse, the regard for the ordinary observances of religious worship less, and religious indifference greater than in Protestant Switzerland."

If from these countries we were to pass to Scotland, we should have a picture of morality too revolting to lay before the general public; yet Scotland may be considered as one of the firmest strongholds of the Protestant religion.

The "Saturday Review" (8th October, 1859, page 421) contains the following :—

> "Scotland presents the spectacle of the most Puritanized and most drunken community on the face of the earth. Nowhere is the strict interpretation of the letter more popular, and nowhere are the free, liberal, and practical influences of the spirit more disregarded. The Sabbath is kept, but the moral law is set aside.
>
> New York is about the most profligate city in the world; in Geneva religion is all but unknown, and in Glasgow, the sons of the Covenanters are the most drunken population on the face of the earth."

The "Times" states that from a Parliamentary paper recently issued at the instance of Dr. Cameron, in the year ending with the 30th of June, 1875, there were in all 65,173 persons arrested for drunkenness in Scotland (38,213 for being drunk and incapable, and 26,960 for being drunk and disorderly).[1] On the

---

[1] It has been stated that most of these were Irish. Whether this is the case or not we do not know; but even admitting that the majority of those arrested were Irish, or descended from Irish parents, we conclude that they must have become con-

question of morality, a leading Presbyterian paper called "The Scotsman" recently wrote as follows:—

"England is nearly twice and Scotland nearly thrice worse than Ireland in the matter of morality. The proportion of illegitimacy is very unequally distributed over Ireland, and the inequalities are such as are rather humbling to us as Protestants, and still more as Presbyterians and Scotchmen.

The division showing the lowest figure is the Western, being substantially the province of Connaught, where about nineteen-twentieths of the population are Celtic and Catholics.

The division showing the highest proportion of illegitimacy is the North-Eastern, which comprises or almost consists of the province of Ulster, where the population is almost equally divided between Protestant and Roman Catholic, and where the great majority of the Protestants are of Scotch blood and of the Presbyterian Church.

The sum of the whole matter is, that semi-Presbyterian and semi-Scotch Ulster is *fully three times more immoral* than wholly Popish and wholly Irish Connaught, which corresponds with wonderful accuracy to the more general fact that Scotland as a whole, is three times more immoral than Ireland as a whole. There is a fact, whatever may be the proper deduction. There is a text whatever may be the sermon. We only suggest that the sermon should have a great deal about charity, self-examination, and humility."

---

taminated by living amongst the Scotch. In any case we know that the Irish in their own country, and under the influence of their clergy, are in a very different condition. A Parliamentary return (No. 437, 1878) affords the latest refutation to the theory that the Irish are more drunken than the English and Scotch. (*See* "Tablet," March 16th, 1878.)

A few years ago a distinguished Protestant writer published a work entitled "Memorandums made in Ireland in the Autumn of 1852," in the course of which he bears frequent and ungrudging testimony to the influence of the confessional as an agent of purity. The writer was Dr. Forbes, one of Her Majesty's physicians. We transcribe some passages from his work which we find quoted in the April number of the "Dublin Review," pp. 437-8:—

"At any rate," says Dr. Forbes, "the result of my inquiries is, that whether right or wrong in a theological or rational point of view, this instrument of confession is, among the Irish of the humbler classes, a direct preservative against certain forms of immorality at least" (vol. ii. p. 81). "Among other charges preferred against confession in Ireland and elsewhere is the facility it affords for corrupting the female mind, and of its actually leading to such corruption. So far from such corruption resulting from the confessional, it is the general belief in Ireland, a belief expressed to me by many trustworthy men in all parts of the country, both by Protestants as well as Catholics, that the singular purity of female life among the lower classes there, is in a considerable degree dependent on this very circumstance" (p. 83). "With a view of testing as far as was practicable the truth of the theory respecting the influence of confession on this branch of morals, I have obtained through the courtesy of the Poor Law Commissioners a return of the number of legitimate and illegitimate children in the workhouses of each of the four provinces of Ireland on a particular day, viz., 27th November, 1852.

It is curious to mark how strikingly the results there conveyed correspond with the confession theory; the proportion of illegitimate children coinciding almost exactly with the relative proportions of the two religions in each province; *being large where the Protestant element is large, and small where it is small,*" &c. &c. (p. 245).

While writing on this subject we may be allowed to quote the testimony of another Protestant writer, Mr. William Gilbert, who, in an article published in "Christian Work," in May, 1864, states that—

" While under the guidance of their priests, Irish women as a class enjoy, and with justice, a reputation for respectability of conduct unsurpassed if equalled by any women in the world."

In Ireland cases of infanticide and baby-farming are almost unknown, whilst in England and Scotland scarcely a day passes by without the papers referring to two or three such occurrences.

The facts we have adduced in these pages are amply sufficient to demonstrate the fallacy of the chain of arguments used by our opponents; but before quitting the subject we will quote the illegitimate births in the poor-houses of the British Isles as given by Dr. Forbes:—

   Ireland   1 illegitimate birth to 16·47 legitimate.
   England 1   „   „ to 1·49   „
   Wales   1   „   „ to 0·46   „

In Ireland the Catholic faith is an actual preservative of private morality, for in Connaught there is only 1 illegitimate birth in 23·53 legitimate, whilst in the north of Ireland, which is a Puritan and Scotch settlement, there is 1 illegitimate birth in 7·26 legitimate. The fact of Irish morality is proverbial, and bears striking contrast to the character of its more wealthy Protestant neighbours; and though many persons may assert that this morality is an idiosyncrasy of the national character, we have no hesitation in affirming it to be the result of Catholic teaching and loyalty to the Church of their ancestors.

A striking testimony to the truth of our remarks has recently been witnessed. Not long ago an assertion of immorality was made in an English newspaper[1] celebrated for its defence of Evangelical truth, against Irish women in general, and the Irish Church in particular, in the following words:—

"The much vaunted chastity of Irish girls is a myth.

In the rural districts of Ireland the priest is the seducer of the parish, and the early improvident marriages of the young people are encouraged by him to conceal his immorality. There is not, and cannot be chastity where Popery reigns."

These observations drew forth from Lord Oranmore a reply which we give *in extenso*:—

[1] "The Rock," a Church of England Family Newspaper, Oct. 5th, 1877.

"SIR,—A letter appears in your number of the 5th instant headed 'Chastity of Irish Girls.' I believe there can be no more uncompromising Protestant, no one more convinced of the evils of the Roman Catholic system than I am. I have taken the 'Rock' since it was published, and admire its straightforward advocacy of Protestant principles, and therefore I the more regret that by some oversight a paragraph so calumnious and untrue should find place in its columns. I have spent much of my life in a Roman Catholic part of Ireland, and know well not only that Irish girls are generally chaste, but that it is quite an exception that Irish priests are (in this sense) immoral men; and yet this paragraph attributes to the whole body adultery with malice aforethought and prepense. The admission of such a paragraph into your journal cannot but bring discredit on the good cause your journal so ably supports.

ORANMORE.

Castle Mac Garrett,
  Co. Mayo."

Such testimony as this in our favour, from one of our strongest opponents, ought to convince every reasonable man of the truth of our previous assertion with reference to the morality of the Irish, even should he refuse to believe in the morality of the great mass of Catholics.

CHAPTER VIII.

THE REFORMATION IN CONNECTION WITH THE DEVELOPMENT OF CIVIL LIBERTIES.

The Reformation wherever it has prevailed has constituted a State Church, and dealt a blow to civil liberty—Civil and political liberty in those countries in which the Reformation did not succeed in establishing a State Church—In those countries where large numbers remained Catholics—Where they branched off into separate bodies—Civil liberty of old standing amongst Catholic nations—Absolutism a modern invention—The Catholic Church alone capable of resisting the dissolving element contained in civil liberty—Practical proofs.

HE assertion is frequently made that the Reformation is conducive to the development of civil liberty, and that Catholicism inevitably leads to despotism and anarchy. People declare that the representative system is the form of government natural to Pro-

testant countries, whilst Catholics are born to absolutism.

Martin, Marshall, and others have written learned works upon the subject which ably demonstrate the following propositions:—

1stly. Wherever the Reformation has prevailed a State Church has been constituted, and a blow has been dealt at civil liberty which has compelled the nation to retrograde instead of advancing in the path of political progress.

2ndly. Civil and political liberties have flourished relatively only in the countries wherein the leaders of the Reformation did not succeed in making a State Church, and in those of whom a great portion of the nation remained Catholic, or formed themselves into separate religious bodies.

3rdly. Civil liberty is of old standing amongst Catholic nations, and absolutism is a modern abuse of power.

4thly. The Catholic Church can alone, in the midst of a nation, offer resistance, in virtue of its religion and by means of its worship, to the dissolving elements contained in civil liberty—which gives expression to every conceivable opinion, and tolerates every imaginable form of worship.

Religious unity maintained by political institutions is an appreciable benefit, and the Catholic Church has never ceased to proclaim this truth; but when Protestants establish State Churches they place themselves in open contradiction with the fundamental principles of their religious rebellion. Amongst Protestants a State Church means the complete subjection of the Church to the State, upon which the Church becomes but the instrument of the State; whereas in Catholic teaching religious unity is not regarded as a temporal means of government, but as a directing principle superior to the State. The Anglican Church, for instance, is a Church created by the State, supported by the State, and kept up for purposes of the State.[1] It is only known in lands where English people are to be found, is as purely English as if heaven were a British colony, and as completely national as if Christ and His Apostles had lived in England and taught only what the English

---

[1] There are doubtless large numbers of clergy and laity in the Anglican communion who would repudiate this idea, but it is one that prevails very extensively amongst men of letters, and includes many of the bishops and dignitaries and a large proportion of laymen in the present day, just as it did in the seventeenth and sixteenth centuries.

the Development of Civil Liberties. 235

Government thought suitable for them to teach. Lord Macaulay[1] writes thus:—

> "The Church of England existed for England alone; it was an institution as purely local as the Court of Common Pleas, and was utterly without machinery for foreign operations. The Church of Scotland existed for Scotland alone, and no one at Lambeth or Edinburgh troubled themselves about what was doing in Poland or Bavaria.
> The spiritual force of Protestantism was a local militia. In England the gaols were filled with men who did not exactly agree with the Court on all points of discipline and doctrine."

Before the sixteenth century civil tolerance in matters of religion was unknown in European politics, except in Rome, where Judaism was always permitted by the authorities from the time of the fall of the Roman Empire.

Outside the Universal Church there can only exist national and particular Churches, confined to those who speak the same language or practise the same customs, and such Churches are invariably intolerant in their political essence. From the time of the coronation of Charles the Great in Rome, Europe was regarded as a Christian republic, practising the worship of the Universal Church, and there was no question

---

[1] "Critical and Historical Essays," by Lord Macaulay.

of introducing any other worship without overthrowing the very constitution of the empire.

The Reformation was effected in the name of liberty of conscience, but it has been in reality the most cruel enemy of liberty, and wherever Lutheranism or Calvinism has secured a footing, there liberty of conscience has been suppressed.

In England and Ireland, Denmark and Sweden, in Brandenbourg and Geneva, the various Reformers looked upon the oppression of the Catholic Church and its destruction as the practical conclusion of their teaching, and inflicted the pain of death on those who practised its doctrines, whilst they maltreated the numerous Protestant sects who ventured to differ from themselves.

Melancthon, the gentlest of the Reformers of that epoch, declared that the Anabaptists should expiate their doctrines by their blood, and called for corporal punishment on the plea that it is the duty of the secular power to announce the Divine law, and to enforce its observation.

Calvin told the Protector Somerset that it was his duty to exterminate by the sword all persons who should oppose the establishment of the Protestant religion.

According to this apostle of "civil tolerance," the punishment of death was desirable, upon the principle that the authority of the Sovereign over the Church cannot be disregarded, without an attempt being directed thereby against the power of the Crown, established by Divine right.

Beza, the friend of Calvin, asserted that the Anti-Trinitarians ought to be hanged without mercy, even if they should retract their belief.

Burleigh, the Minister of Queen Elizabeth, held as a principle that the security of the State would be endangered if two forms of religion were tolerated.

Even the Chancellor Bacon thought that a government had reached the ultimate limits of tolerance when it was content with exacting an external adhesion to the established religion of the country, without penetrating to the conscience.

It is impossible for us to criticize with too great severity the hypocrisy of the authors of a religious revolution, professedly undertaken for the purpose of establishing a reign of freedom for the human mind.

Catholics were at least faithful to the political traditions of their country and the naturally intolerant principles of their faith when they defended themselves, in preventing by the aid of the civil power the introduction of heresy; but the case assumes an entirely different aspect when Protestants act in a similar way.

With Catholicism, which is based on the principle of absolute certainty, against which it is theoretically impossible to suppose any right, intolerance, however much it may be deemed worthy of blame, cannot be styled illogical, whilst with those whose principle is freedom of opinion and private judgment it is not only bad in itself, but unreasonable and contrary to their own premises.

Some of the Reformers went so far as to contest the right of sovereignty to those princes who did not admit their heresies, and declared that their deposition would be lawful and necessary. Knox, the great Scotch Reformer, made himself very remarkable in the application of this doctrine. Luther stirred up the peasantry against their rulers, in a writing in which he proclaims with loud voice the liberties of the Gospel.

When the war of the peasants threatened the existence of the Protestant principalities, the protectors of Luther begged him to intervene, whereupon he fulminated another writing to curse the peasants for having so well put into execution the conclusions of

the Development of Civil Liberties. 239

his first work. These two contradictory statements are worthy of being placed by the side of the famous dispensation that was granted to cover the bigamy of the Landgrave of Hesse.

After these few general considerations, let us cast a rapid glance over the various Protestant nations and the civil institutions which their religious novelties inspire.

In Sweden we find an inconceivable amount of intolerance and immorality. One law ordained that every man who remained more than a year out of the communion of the national Established Church should be exiled from the country; another ordained that anyone who should make use of expressions (in theological matters) calculated to shock the national Church and refuse to retract them, should suffer exile.

The King is still considered the supreme sovereign and inspector, as well as the earthly master of the Church: he unites in his person the highest temporal and spiritual power.

His authority over the Church is administered by the Royal Chancellorship, which has for its president the Minister of Public Affairs.

Gustavus Wasa informed the inhabitants of Helsingland that if they refused to become Lutherans at his command he would order an opening to be cut in the ice on the Lake of Deel and have them all drowned.

The sword, the prison, exile, and exorbitant fines have always been regarded in Sweden as practices of civil liberty and toleration.

Charles IX. and his son Gustavus Adolphus beheaded the Catholics. At the close of the seventeenth century and the beginning of the eighteenth, when Ulstadius, Schaefer, Ulhagius, and Molin rejected the doctrine of mere justification by faith, and taught the necessity of good works, the first was condemned to a prison, in which he languished for the space of thirty years, reflecting upon the tolerance of the Swedish Church; the second and third were put to death, and the latter was exiled from the country.

The introduction of Protestantism into the northern part of Europe was organized by a coalition of laymen who coveted the possession of the goods of the Church, of Kings, and noblemen who desired to exercise unrestrained power, of regulars weary of their rule of continence and fasting, and of seculars who were desirous of legalizing their immorality.

The Reformation should be studied, in the places where it prevailed, by the light of the history of the sixteenth century, and with the knowledge and under-

the Development of Civil Liberties. 241

standing of ancient institutions and modern progress. The masses of the people were in every instance deceived. In Sweden, Gustavus Wasa always refused to admit that he was introducing new doctrines, and fifty years after the official introduction of Lutheranism many of the people still imagined that they were Catholics. It was only by slow degrees that the masses became conscious that they were in a Lutheran country.

The Protestant Church in Sweden began as an instrument of government and police administration—"an appendage," according to the words of the Swedish historian Geijer, "to the military and civil authorities," and it remains to this day an instrument of tyranny and oppression.

Although theoretically the royal power was constituted conformably to the principles of the Renaissance and the Apostles of the Reformation, on an absolute basis, it was practically made subservient to the wishes of the large class of powerful nobles. Sweden is still asleep, and if it were not for Linnéus, Berzelius, and Geijer would at the present day be as little known as Maracaibo. Such is the effect of Protestantism, after a trial of three hundred years in the soil of the holy Eric IX., and no one can possibly claim for Sweden a place in the picture of civil liberty.

Denmark is little better. Molesworth, who was thoroughly acquainted with the history of Protestantism in the north of Europe, wrote thus as early as the year 1692:—

"The Roman Catholic religion with its supreme head in Rome maintains perpetual opposition to the doctrine of unlimited political power, but the Lutherans are on the contrary invariably subject to the State, and reduced to the condition of servitude. From the time that the people of Northern Europe exchanged their old religion for a better one, they may be considered as having lost their liberty."

In Denmark Lutheranism was completely triumphant, and what was the result? Barthold, a Protestant historian of Berlin, tells it in these words:—

"The peasant was again reduced to a state of serfdom, the citizen was deprived of every means of defence, and sank under the weight of civil and military oppression.

The King and the nobles shared the sovereignty, and the masses of the people, and even the children of the clergy became mere serfs."

The nobility appropriated to themselves not only the revenues of the Church, but also the free-holdings of the peasants.

Allen, in his "History of Denmark," which has

been recognized by the Academy of Copenhagen as the best work on the subject, writes thus :—

"The tenants of the great ecclesiastical domains were compelled to exchange the gentle administration of the clergy for the crushing despotism of the nobles. Fines and other hardships were arbitrarily multiplied, and the peasants were treated with severity. Agriculture, which was thus forcibly abandoned, fell below the level that it had attained during the Middle Ages. The population decreased in numbers, and the country was covered with deserted habitations."

The civil rights of the clergy and middle classes were in their turn attacked, and eight or nine hundred nobles reigned supreme over a country which had rejected the apostolic liberty of the Church. Christian IV. (1588-1648) made an attempt to break down this wall of absolutism, but without success.

Frederick III. and his successors proclaimed themselves as absolute Sovereigns. A law was passed in the year 1665 which declared it desirable that the King should be bound by no oath or obligation, but that his authority should be paramount. Let anyone contrast these proceedings with the oath taken by the Catholic Kings of Aragon before the period of the Renaissance and the obligations incurred by the Kings of Castile, and consider in what way the Reformation may be regarded as a return to civil liberty.

Let them examine the charters of the Basque Countries and of Flanders, and see whether their forefathers were more ignorant of the principles of true liberty than themselves.

In 1702 Frederick VI. abolished serfdom to replace it by another form of tyranny, that of attaching the peasant to the soil. Schools were few, and in 1766 it may be said that primary instruction was *nil*. At the close of the eighteenth century scarcely one person in twenty could read, and it was not until the year 1805 that personal liberty was for the first time conceded to 20,000 families of serfs. In the year 1714 the Bishops of Norway addressed the following petition to King Frederick IV., which shows to what a pitch of degradation the kingdom had sunk. They say: "With the exception of a small number of people, between ourselves and our pagan ancestors there is the single difference that we bear the name of Christians."

The Provincial Diet which was re-established by Frederick VI. did not restrain the absolutism of royalty, but acted in a subservient spirit of fear. In the year 1839 Laing, in his "Notes of a Traveller," says:—

"Since the Danes are completely passive as regards politics, and never raise their voices to discuss their own affairs, they remain, in spite of the large number of excellent ordonnances decreed by the government, in the same condition as they were in 1660.

They are two centuries behind such nations as the Scotch, the Dutch, and the Belgians, in comparison with whom they may be placed as regards their population and general position."

In Mecklenburg serfdom was only abolished in the year 1829; in Pomerania the States-General were suppressed almost immediately after the accession of the first Protestant Duke; and in Hanover and Brunswick the States-General disappeared before the absolutism of their respective sovereigns, where history would find little to record were it not for the great memory of Leibnitz. Let us see how civil liberty was interpreted in the Electorate of Brandenbourg.

The reader will doubtless remember how the principles of the Reformers were but insensibly instilled amongst the people, and how Prussia was torn from the Teutonic order that possessed it.

During the whole of the sixteenth century a certain hesitation is manifest among the princes of Hohenzollern in their conduct towards their subjects. The weak and vacillating Duke Albert, the Elector Joachim, and his son George alike needed the assistance of the States-General by reason of their misdeeds.

From the beginning of the seventeenth century the convocation of the States was suspended, and from the year 1656 no further Diet was summoned. Whilst the French were devastating the Palatinate, according to the military custom of that period, the great Elector laid waste the administration of his own States. The government of Prussia was in no respect different from that of Sweden or Denmark, either as regards its despotism or its brutality.

According to the words of the historian Stenzel, Prussia was on the high road to becoming one of those Asiatic States wherein despotism stifles all that is noble and beautiful.

Military pursuits and the passions of the chase were the two ideas of the sovereign which the nation was called upon to countenance and provide for—pursuits which exhausted its resources and its life. The peasants were ground down under a crushing servitude as galling as it was despotic.

Frederick William I. (1713-1740) carried out the spirit of absolutism to the minutest details. Under his ignoble reign the Protestant clergy were given less consideration than the lowest rank of officers in the army.

No writer with any regard for truth can put forward Frederick II. as a protector of civil liberty. Toellner quotes a writing[1] of his in which this disciple of Voltaire reveals the fact that the principal cause of his contempt for the Christian religion lay in the disgust he felt for ecclesiastical history as put before him by the Protestants. He saw nought in it but a stage representation played by mischief-makers and hypocrites at the expense of the masses, who were made their dupes and victims.

Carlyle, in his celebrated work on Frederick the Great, draws a striking picture of the open dislike that monarch displayed for all the primary doctrines of the Reformation, and the despotic and tyrannical disposition of his character. If men carefully observe what is passing before their eyes in the present day in Italy, France, Belgium, and other countries, they must be struck with the fact that in every case the various Liberal governments that have exercised power have curtailed civil liberty, and deprived large numbers of those for whom they legislate of their most sacred and inviolable rights. Unless "civil liberty" is made to consist in mere hatred of, and

[1] Preface of the work entitled "Abridgment of Fleury's Ecclesiastical History," Berne, 1869. M. de Prades was the author of the work, and Frederick II. wrote the preface.

declamation against the Catholic Church, it is evident that from the departure of the Duke of Alva down to the French Revolution of 1789, Belgium enjoyed much more freedom than the Low Countries, which were Calvinist. The recent works of Professor Poullet, of Louvain, throw floods of light on this point of history.

Niebuhr, the Protestant historian, declares that the Reformed Church in Holland was grossly tyrannical, and that it cannot be lauded either for intellect or good judgment; also that Calvinism everywhere alike, whether in Holland, Scotland, or Geneva, manifested a thirst for blood equivalent at least to that of the Inquisition, and has in no one instance exhibited the merits of Catholicism.

The absolutism of the House of Orange was impeded by the firm adhesion of a large portion of the populace to the Catholic Church, and by the formation of numerous dissident sects. The Catholics, deprived of all political rights, served as a passive means to render impossible the omnipotence of the dominant Church.

Nevertheless, with regard to civil liberties, Holland presents an aspect more consoling than that of any other Protestant country. Calvinism was the religion of the State, but the States-General guaranteed, at different epochs and in different degrees, a certain amount of liberty towards such dissident sects as Armenians, Lutherans, and Mennonites, that had come from other parts. Catholicism alone, though it embraced two-fifths of the population, was mercilessly oppressed until the present generation. The States-General protected Spinosa and Bayle, though they proscribed the religious liberties of the co-religionists of Fénelon and Malebranche.

The worst productions of the literature of the eighteenth century were allowed to circulate in Holland, and liberty of the press was practically alone denied to Catholics.

England, under Elizabeth, furnishes a most striking example of the inauguration of liberty by the Protestant Reformation. In this reign not only the episcopal office, but also ecclesiastical doctrine was subjected to the will of the sovereign.

Hallam[1] writes thus of the Anglican Church in 1566: "The novel theory of ecclesiastical authority resolved all its spiritual as well as temporal powers into the royal supremacy," a statement which is confirmed by English lawyers. Blackstone, for instance,

[1] Hallam's "Constitutional History," vol. i. p. 100.

says: "The authority heretofore exercised by the Pope is now annexed to the Crown by the statutes of Henry VIII., Edward, and Elizabeth."[1]

The Anglican Church is in complete subjection to the State. Such are the words of the leading ecclesiastical papers in England of the present day—words which have been amply verified by recent legislation. The "Public Worship Regulation Act" is an example of this, an Act hurried through a Parliament composed of men of every shade of belief, in one session, and then forced upon a body of clergy who were certainly not in favour of it. It is worthy of notice also, that Convocation, which may in a certain sense be considered as the mouthpiece of the Anglican clergy, was not even consulted on the matter.

The tolerant legislation for Ireland is so well known that in a short work like the present it is unnecessary to dwell much on it, but for the benefit of those who are under the delusion that Protestantism produces civil liberty we will quote a few of the penal laws, which prove the fact that children were torn away from their parents' protection, priests were hung or exiled, and those who refused to conform to the wishes of the British Government were made serfs in

[1] Blackstone's "Commentaries," vol. iii. p. 67.

the Development of Civil Liberties. 251

their own land. In England for three hundred years Catholics were hunted like wild beasts, and the punishment of death was inflicted on a priest for saying the Mass.

In the year 1695 the following laws were enacted :—

1. The Catholic Peers were deprived of their right to sit in Parliament.

2. Catholic gentlemen were forbidden to be elected as members of Parliament.

3. Catholics were denied the liberty of voting, and were excluded from all offices of trust and all remunerative employment.

4. They were fined £60 a month for absence from Protestant worship.

5. They were forbidden to travel five miles from their houses, to keep arms, to maintain suits at law, or to be guardians or executors.

6. Any four justices of the peace could, without further trial, banish any man for life if he refused to attend the Protestant service.

7. Any two justices of the peace could call any man over sixteen before them, and if he refused to abjure the Catholic religion, could bestow his property on the next of kin.

8. No Catholic could employ a Catholic schoolmaster to educate his children; and if he sent his child abroad for education he was subject to a fine of £100, and the child could not inherit any property in England or Ireland.

9. Any Catholic priest who came to the country might be hanged.

10. Any Protestant suspecting any other Protestant of holding property in trust for a Catholic might file a bill against the suspected trustee and take the estate from him.

11. Any Protestant seeing a Catholic tenant-at-will on a farm which, in his opinion, yielded one-third more than the yearly rent, might enter on that farm, and, by simply swearing to the fact, take possession.

12. Any Protestant might take away the horse of a Catholic, no matter how valuable, by simply paying him £5.

13. Horses and waggons belonging to Catholics were in all cases to be seized for the use of the Militia.

14. Any Catholic gentleman's child who became a Protestant could at once take possession of his father's property.

the Development of Civil Liberties. 253

The 13th of Charles II., commonly called "The Corporation Act," excluded Catholics from offices in cities and corporations.

The 25th Charles II., commonly called "The Test Act," excluded them from all civil and military offices.

The 30th Charles II. prevented them from taking part in the legislation of the country.

An Act of William and Mary prevented the use of the Parliamentary franchise.

The horrors of the penal code were slightly relaxed in 1778, when American agitation and English fear permitted Catholics to hold property on leases for lives, but still the vast majority of the nation was excluded from the franchises, offices, and honours of the State, not on account of any moral or political delinquency, but merely on account of its religion. The whole history of the persecutions which Catholics have endured at the hands of Protestants of every denomination is one of the most curious phases of human perversity that the philosopher can find to study.

The Rev. Dr. Leland, a Protestant minister, writes as follows[1] on the plantation of Ulster, which James I.

[1] Leland, book iv. chap. 8.

and his successor not only devised, but carried into effect:—

"They obtained commissions of inquiry into defective titles and grants of concealed lands and rents belonging to the Crown, the great benefit of which was to accrue to the projector, whilst the King was contented with an inconsiderable proportion of the concealment, or a small advance of rent.

Discoverers were everywhere busily employed in finding out flaws in men's titles to their estates. The old pipe-rolls were searched to find the original rents with which they had been charged, the patent rolls in the Tower of London were ransacked for the ancient grants, no means of industry or devices of craft were left untried to force the possessors to accept of new grants at an advanced rent. In general men were either conscious of defects in their titles, or alarmed at the trouble and expense of a contest with the Crown, or fearful of the issue of such a contest at a time and in a country where the prerogative was highly strained and strenuously supported by the judges. There are not wanting proofs of the most iniquitous practices of hardened cruelty, of vile perjury, and scandalous subornation, employed to despoil the fair and unoffending proprietor of his inheritance."

Unheard-of confiscations were made in the northern parts, upon grounds of plots and conspiracies never proved upon their supposed authors. The original scheme of depopulation was never lost sight of, and a regular series of operations was carried on by special commissions and inquisitions, first under pretence of tenures and then of titles in the Crown, until the original inhabitants were almost completely exterminated. Parliament passed a law vesting the entire land of six counties in the Crown, the property of Irishmen, and the King immediately distributed upwards of 385,000 acres to his followers.[1] There were three divisions made of the spoils—first, to English and Scotch, who were to plant their portions of territory with English and Scotch tenants; secondly, to servitors in Ireland—that is, to persons employed under the Government, who might take English or Irish tenants at their choice; thirdly, to the natives of those countries, who were to be freeholders. Catholics and persons of Irish descent, who were known by the name of "mere Irish," were altogether excluded from this part of the country.

Such was the Plantation of Ulster, and, to show the spirit in which it was made, we give the following "Articles," extracted from the orders and conditions of the Plantation of Ulster:—

(7.) "The said undertakers, their heirs and assigns, shall not alien or demise their portions, or any part thereof, to the mere Irish, or to such persons as will not take the oath which the said undertakers are bound to take by the said article, and to that end a proviso shall be inserted in the letters patent."

(8.) "The said undertakers shall not alien their portions during five years next after the date of their letters patent, but in this

[1] Leland, book iv. chap. 8.

manner—viz., one third part in fee farm," &c. " But after the said five years they shall be at liberty to alien to all persons except the mere Irish." (Harris's "Hibernica," p. 66.)

The documents here cited give but a faint idea of the extreme misery created by this plantation. The administration of the law was quite consistent with the temper of the times, and the Protestant Bishop Burnet does not hesitate to denounce the partiality and injustice that were exhibited.[1]

Scotland furnishes us with an example of a country entirely given up to the spirit of intolerance. Lord Clarendon, speaking of the Scotch in 1660, says: "Their whole religion consists in hatred of popery." Few "apostles of tolerance" pushed a hatred of truth to such a pitch as John Knox, who declared that it rightly appertained to the civil power to regulate everything connected with religion. He issued a warrant of death against anyone who should celebrate the holy sacrifice of the Mass twice. An ecclesiastical tyranny was established under his direction of which it is now hardly possible to form a conception. In Chambers's "Domestic Annals" we find the statement that the private life of each individual was subjected to investigation like that exercised in the East.

[1] Bishop Burnet's "Life of Bishop Bedell."

The despotism exercised by the ruling authorities in Scotland exceeded that in Geneva, the birthplace of Calvinism and centre of revolutionary intrigue.

In 1713, Parliament, aided by the Crown, compelled the Scotch Calvinists to tolerate the introduction of an Episcopal Church. The year 1735 marks the first approach to any kind of liberty in Scotland, and then for the first time the poor Highlanders who had remained steadfast to the Catholic Church obtained permission to come down from their mountainous abodes in order to practise the religion of their ancestors, and to teach England the spiritual power of the faith of Edward the Confessor.

The anarchy of the various Protestant denominations of the United States of America is well known, but we will recall for some of our readers the memorable fact that since the era of Luther the only sincere attempt to establish a system of religious liberty previous to Washington was made by the Catholics.

As we have mentioned in a previous chapter, Maryland was founded by Lord Baltimore as a refuge for persons of every religious belief, and the fundamental principle was laid down that there should be perfect liberty for all.

The Puritan party, the descendants of those who loudly preached the right of private judgment and liberty of conscience, devastated this noble territory and destroyed every trace of its former freedom.

In a study so brief as this we cannot do more than point out what is most important, but we think that what we have pointed out is amply sufficient to prove the correctness of our original propositions—viz., that Protestantism has destroyed civil liberty wherever it has gained the ascendency, and that politically it has produced a retrograde movement in the nations who have been subjected to its influence. In Catholic nations, on the contrary, liberty is of old standing, and absolutism is completely modern.

England is a living witness of this statement, and England is the country which in the present day gives the clearest idea of what the nations of Europe would have been if Protestantism and the Pagan liberalism of the Renaissance had not stifled in them the growth of institutions dating from the thirteenth century.

Every civil liberty except that of worship, which dates only from our own time, existed in Great Britain previous to the Reformation, and Great Britain alone of European nations may be said to have escaped the effects of the Renaissance. Although Great Britain severed itself from the outward unity of the Church, she did it apparently in a manner not sufficiently complete to satisfy the Neo-Protestant school of modern liberals.

The English episcopal system is in its present form the denial of the fundamental principle of Protestantism.

Nearly all the fruitful undertakings of Englishmen date from Catholic times, and are essentially Catholic, and every danger that England carries within her bosom arises from the convulsions of the religious revolution brought about by Henry VIII. France, Spain, Austria, Portugal, and Italy escaped the consequences of the Reformation to fall into the generative errors of the Renaissance which produced Cæsarism, or its modern form of irreligious radicalism and infidelity. Their misfortune was not so great as that of the nations that became Protestant, but their suffering has nevertheless been long and serious.

Catholic nations, to become free again, require "the liberty of the children of God," the liberty that permits them the free and unrestrained exercise of their religion, and the civil right to put forth publicly its worship and its doctrines.

Protestant nations can only become free by ceasing

to be Protestant and forfeiting the illusory promises of the Reformation. This double phenomenon is very clearly discernible in our day.

Ubi Petrus, ibi ecclesia. In the political language of the day we might translate these well-known words thus: "Where the Pope is, there is liberty."

Outside of Christianity there can be no real civil liberty; the liberty that preceded it was based upon slavery, which Aristotle, the prince of Anti-Christian philosophy, justified from a rational point of view.

Christian truth in its integrity is only to be found in the Universal Church, and without this truth there is no genuine liberty.

"Cognoscetis veritatem et veritas liberavit vos."—"You know the truth, and truth shall make you free."

If men would carry their intellects a step beyond their miserable differences on questions of persons and distinctions of words, and study with care and diligence the history of the Universal Church from the martyrdom of St. Peter down to the present day, they would realize the truth of our assertion that the Church has always been the guardian and protector of true liberty.

During the past eighteen centuries the Church Catholic Apostolic and Roman has been opposed by all the errors which the spirit of evil is capable of fomenting; it has been triumphant over all, from the time of the Jews who stoned St. Stephen down to the year 1871, when the Communists of Paris butchered the Archbishop of Paris and scores of the clergy in cold blood.

That the gates of hell have not prevailed and cannot prevail against the Church of Peter is a fact which all Catholics admit with certainty; but it may not be useless to recount for the benefit of others a few historical events to demonstrate the truth of it in the past.

The distinction of the two powers (temporal and spiritual) in scholastic language, and the source of civil liberty were revealed to mankind by the Gospel, and were completely unknown to paganism. The Christians, more instructed and more humble of spirit, knew through the means of faith that this distinction of the two powers was to be henceforth the condition of social life, and the Christians of the present day entertain no doubt but that it will remain until the consummation of time, until the day when all earthly distinctions will be removed to make way for a truth eternally one.

But as many may doubt, we purpose to prove by

the outward history of the Church that she alone has been able to maintain, side by side with the purity of faith in Christ Jesus, the complete integrity of civil liberty.

When St. Peter, the fisherman of Galilee, arrived in Rome, which he calls Babylon (1 Peter v. 13), the Roman Empire was in the might of its power, and offered to the world a spectacle of corruption and an amount of unparalleled despotism that would horrify our contemporaries. The works of Tacitus and Juvenal give evidence of that which the early Christians had to undergo, and we their descendants possess their living history in the Acts of the Martyrs.

From the crucifixion of the first Bishop of Rome, on the Vatican mount, until the proclamation of the edict of universal tolerance published by Constantine in 313, the blood of Catholics flowed to expiate the infamies of the ancient world. Civil liberty issued forth from the catacombs, and the words of Julian the Apostate, "Galilean, thou hast conquered," convey the expression of unwilling testimony in their favour.

Then followed the invasions of the barbaric hordes, and by whom was their destructive wave arrested? Was it by the mighty Roman Empire or the Church; was it by the sons of Theodosius or by Pope Leo?

the Development of Civil Liberties. 263

When the Roman Empire of the West disappeared, in the year 476, in the cradle of a child, Romulus Augustulus, the Roman Church had already brought to the savage tribes of the north of Europe the torch of faith, the only true light of civil society.

" Christians must not overthrow error by the use of violence or constraint, but by persuasion, instruction, love, and charity." Such are the words of the great St. John of Chrysostom.

From the reign of Pope Gregory the Great to that of Nicholas the Great, this work of spiritual sanctification and civil culture continued without interruption. St. Gregory was the civilizer of England, and St. Nicholas sent St. Anascharius to be the Apostle of Northern Europe.

During the first nine centuries the Arians, the Manicheans, and the Nestorians appeared and disappeared, crumbled in their turn into dust by the rigours of an Asiatic despotism.

The fate of the schism of Photius, of the Greek Church, since its separation from the See of Peter, is well known throughout Christendom.

Its condition might be styled Byzantinism, whereby we designate at the same time a society without civil liberty and an ecclesiastical body without expansion.

The Russian Church of to-day, under the iron heel of the Czar, and the Church in Greece, nominally under the jurisdiction of the Patriarch of Constantinople, are both practically at the mercy of their respective sovereigns, and are as purely national and creatures of the State as the existing Establishment in England. The other portions of the Greek Church to be found in the dominions of the Sultan of Turkey cannot be considered as the pioneers or champions of civil liberty, though less ground down by the secular power than their brethren in Greece and Russia.

Those portions of the Greek and Armenian Churches that are in communion with the See of Peter are alone able to resist successfully the encroachments of the State, and stand out in noble contrast to those around them.

When Charlemagne laid the foundations of the Holy Roman Empire of Teutonic race, he was crowned by the Sovereign Pontiff, and undertook the responsibility of the maintenance of civil liberty throughout the West, which was at that epoch perpetually threatened by the invasion of new hordes of barbarians and the ravages of neighbouring tribes. Under the feeble successors of that great Emperor civil authority was threatened with a new series of dangers, produced by the abuses of the feudal system, political anarchy, and serfage in all its debasing forms, suggesting the right of the strong to oppress the weak, and without the Catholic Church, civil liberty would have been completely annihilated. After this followed the communal era: and amongst the first protectors of communal freedom we find a Pope (Alexander II.). It was the Church of Rome that opposed the Cæsarism of the German Sovereigns when they attempted to transplant into Europe the laws, customs, and morals of Constantinople.

Without the faithfulness of the Catholic hierarchy, without the indomitable energy of the bishops and monks, and without the supreme resistance of the successors of St. Peter, such as that of Gregory VII., Innocent III., Boniface VIII., and many more, the coalition of the partisans of Cæsarism in the Middle Ages would have been triumphant throughout the length and breadth of the Empire.

On the failure of Teutonic Cæsarism in the thirteenth century, the cause was taken up by the jurists and men of letters. In order to realize the immense danger of such a line of action for the civil liberty of Europe, it suffices to read the consultations of the Bolognese doctors who were brought to the

Diet of Roncaglia by Frederic Barbarossa, and the civil code written by Peter Desvignes for Frederick II. at Naples.

The maternal solicitude of the Roman Church again delivered Christendom from these fresh dangers.

When the partial success of Protestantism had broken up the moral unity of the great Christian republic, the principle admitted in the empire as to the distinction of the two powers had no further defence than the personal or hereditary power of the House of Hapsburg. The Church, however, persisted in her immutability, and to her protection do we owe our preservation from the decline with which the Pagan materialism of the Renaissance, the despotism of the Protestant princes, the rigorism of the Jansenists, and the invasions of the Turks threatened the whole continent of Europe.

But though Europe did not entirely escape the deep wounds of the troublous era of the sixteenth century, and though it had to witness the corruption of a large number of salutary civil institutions (the fruit of the Middle Ages), and though it had to see the re-introduction of the theories and practices of the Imperial Roman law, our Catholic ancestors were able, owing to the firm attitude of the Church, to discover a *modus*

the Development of Civil Liberties. 267

vivendi which prevented them from descending to the low moral standard of such countries as Sweden, Norway, Denmark, Prussia, and Scotland.

The Turks do not appear to us in this the close of the nineteenth century in the light of formidable adversaries, but the case was very different with our forefathers at the time they added to the suffrages of the Litanies the following invocation : " From the fury of the Turks deliver us, O Lord ;" but we can judge from Africa, Asia, and the Balkan peninsula of the nefarious consequences that arose from the political greatness of the Osmanlis with reference to the civil liberty of the peoples they conquered, and what power it was that sheltered Europe from the effects of this corrosive influence.

In the year 732 a Catholic army under the command of a Frank chief, Charles Martel, arrested the march of the Mussulman at Poictiers.

For seven centuries the Catholics of Spain, as we have already mentioned in a former chapter, distinguished themselves in the defence of civil liberty by combating the Mahometans that were established in their country. The victory of Lepanto was owing to St. Pius V., and it was the Catholic people of Austria, the line of the Hapsburgs, John Sobieski and the Poles who forced the Turks to halt on the Danube, and saved Northern Europe from the fate of Herzegovina and Bosnia in the present day.

The mention of Poland leads to a slight digression. The civil liberties, the secular institutions, the independence of the religion, and even the name of this unfortunate country were wrested from it in a time of peace by a coalition headed by Lutherans and schismatics. Harris, afterwards the first Lord Malmesbury, who witnessed this international crime, having given an account of it to his Government, received the following laconic reply from Lord Suffolk, the Minister of Foreign Affairs: "It is a curious transaction." One man alone in Europe protested; that man was the Pope. "*Ubi Petrus, ibi libertas*"—"Where the Pope is, there is liberty."

We have sketched the outlines of the picture of the ruin caused by Protestantism in civil society, and we might now add that of the noble resistance made by the Roman Church to the excesses of modern Cæsarism, with its accompanying and diversified errors of Gallicanism, Josephism, Sans-culottism, and Bonapartism. The greatest despot of our times met with only two invincible forces that resisted him, the Catholic Spaniards and Pope Pius VII.

Modern liberalism, the Cæsarism of the nineteenth century, is confronted by only one insurmountable object, the immovable rock of the Catholic Church, which will triumph in the end over this form of error as it has done over every other.

We do not propose to enter into the development of this subject, which would carry us beyond the limits of this work, but, after having accumulated facts and proofs, we must be permitted to close the discussion by an assertion which is being at the present moment visibly demonstrated by passing events in Germany, in Switzerland, and other countries. Anti-Catholic liberalism threatens the civil liberty of modern Europe with an immense danger, against which there is no remedy save in the practice of the Catholic religion. If our opponents were to read attentively the encyclical letters *Mirari vos* and *Quanta cura*, they would find in them nothing that sincere reason could reject.

Either the whole structure of Christianity is false or these encyclicals are the expression of supreme truth.[1] Let them detach from them the ancient style of the Pontifical Chancellery, as people are willing

---

[1] *See* an article of great power, entitled "The Future of Faith," by W. H. Mallock, "Contemporary Review."

enough to do in the case of a decree emanating from one of the ancient courts of England; let them place themselves on the ground of absolute right (the only one which the Pope considers); let them remember that the Pope, when he treats of such subjects, speaks for all centuries; let them consider the contemporary errors which have called forth these doctrinal decisions; let them read over the details, and reflect seriously and humbly, as an attentive, instructed, and learned mind should reflect in every circumstance of life, and then come to an impartial conclusion.

The Popes of our time, in pronouncing doctrinal judgments, which ignorance or hatred disfigures and distorts; in defining, with the authority attached to the science of the Church of Christ, now eighteen hundred years old, the absolute conditions of Christian truth in its relations with civil and political law—the Popes of our time in thus acting have rendered to our era a service which will draw down upon them the blessings of posterity.

We are aware that persons exist who claim to make capital out of these judgments, admirable as they are for wisdom and a clear insight into the human mind, and we are aware that under the veil of certain religious appearances deception, the narrow-mindedness of party spirit, and the pride of men who forget that faith is the gift of God are often concealed.

We are aware of the maledictions uttered against everything good by a class of malcontents who would have held the same language in the time of St. Francis of Assisi and St. Dominic, but nothing that we can see or hear can prevent us from admiring the resplendent light which the Church sheds forth on all sides. Those who cannot see this light must indeed be smitten with judicial blindness.

"*Ubi Petrus, ibi libertas*"—"Where the Pope is, there is liberty." Political absolutism is contrary to the essence of the Church. The history of the present period would suffice to prove that Catholics suffer revolutions, but do not create them. Wherever despotism and revolution have prevailed it is the liberals who have reaped the fruits, even if they have not been the authors, on the pretext that Catholics were seditious. Nero beheaded St. Paul and crucified St. Peter, declaring that they had provoked civil war in the empire. There is an excellent fable entitled "The Wolf and the Sheep," in which the same dialectic is made use of.

Biblical and philosophical rationalism took their

rise in Protestant Prussia. Renan is at least a disciple of Strauss, and this filiation is not only a thing of our day.

In our estimation a perfect civil society would be that wherein the Catholic religion should be sincerely put in practice by all its members. Proclus used to say: "The philosopher does not bind himself to such and such a national form of worship; he is alien to no particular form, because he is the high priest of the universe." The prefect Symmachus said: "What does it signify by what road we arrive at truth? It is a thing so mysterious that there must be many roads leading to it." It is evident that if civil society is to be moulded upon subjectivism, it must tend, as far as politics are concerned, to the anarchy of M. Proudhon. The civil society which would take the Catholic religion for its model does not submit to an absolute human authority.

The Pontifical authority in the Church is no more than that of the father in the family. These two authorities—the one natural, the other spiritual—are tempered, the first by love and by the civil law, the second by the grace of God and the constitution of the Church. Since the influence naturally exercised by the dominant worship of a people upon the form

the Development of Civil Liberties. 273

of civil society is great, great religious care is necessary for a Catholic to maintain the necessary distinction of the two powers. The analogy between the form of the religious society and the form of the civil society is not necessary; for the source of the two societies is different, and this difference is the religious guarantee of civil liberty.

The form of religious society is divine, and determined by the will of its Divine Founder, but the form of civil society (aristocracy, democracy, monarchy, &c.) is of human origin. St. Thomas, whom modern liberals would probably style an Ultramontane, looked upon monarchy, tempered by aristocracy and democracy, as the most desirable form of government, whilst Bossuet, the leading character of the Gallican school, was absolutist in politics.

Since the conversion of Constantine, and more recently since the coronation of Charlemagne as temporal head of the Christian republic, civil society, under the maternal nurture of the Church, had followed a development which the false ideas of the Renaissance and the Protestant revolution of the sixteenth century have ruined. Since the sixteenth century European society has been morally broken up, and the institutions of centuries, which the people had gradually and with great difficulty obtained, have had no further development; they have, on the contrary, become corrupted, have fallen into disuse, or have been wrested with violence from the people.

All this is the work of the Renaissance and the Reformation. The French revolution of 1789, in substituting, pure rationalism for the subjective form of Christianity that the sixteenth century had produced, was no innovator, but it gave to the revolution of the Reformation an application much more dangerous to Protestantism than to Catholicism. Protestant governments had from the sixteenth century suppressed the civil liberties of Catholics, whereas the French revolution professed, at least in theory, to give freedom to every form of worship. The positive consequences have been, renewed life and vigour amongst Catholics and a corresponding decline and weakening amongst the official Protestant sects.

Without the aid of the secular arm all forms of Protestantism based upon the subjectivism of individual reason must crumble away into atoms, whilst the great Universal Church can not only dispense with the support of governments, but can, if need be, return to the catacombs, and assume the same attitude as she did in the first ages of the Church. The more she is persecuted the more will she become strengthened. "*Sanguis martyrum semen Christianorum*"—"The blood of martyrs is the seed of the Church," and this truth has become an acknowledged fact in history.

Many persons are fully persuaded that we are approaching a condition of things in religion very much akin to that of the fourth century, but the greater the trials and difficulties of the Church the more certain are we of her eventual triumph.

Christ's promise cannot fail, "Lo, I am with you always, even unto the consummation of time;" and Catholics are perfectly content to endure whatever sufferings and persecution their Lord thinks it necessary for the Church to undergo, in order that "she may become bright and clean, without spot or blemish or any such thing." The adversaries of the Church imagine, in their ignorance and hatred, that since she does not admit a faith that is purely individual and subjective, she must finally be destroyed; they imagine that, like a human institution, as soon as she is deprived of her political prerogatives and earthly support, and left without temporal means of defence against the attacks of unbelievers, she must succumb.

They are already beginning to see they were mistaken. The Church has shone with a new lustre precisely in those countries of England, America, Germany, and Switzerland where everything that human means could devise had been put in force against her. They are themselves alarmed at the progress she has made.

The Catholics in the beginning of the present century stood as one to every two hundred of the whole population of the American Republic. The ratio of Catholics now is one to six or seven of the inhabitants; and before the end of this century the assertion has frequently been made, that they will outnumber all other believers in Christianity throughout the States. Such an assertion is no fanciful statement, but one based on a careful study of statistics.

The spirit, the tendencies, and the form of political government inherited by the people of the United States are strongly Saxon; yet there are no better citizens and no more intelligent and devoted subjects in the Republic than the seven millions of Catholics. Catholicism is the only persistently progressive religious element in the States.

That the Catholic Church flourishes wherever there is honest freedom, and wherever human nature has its

the Development of Civil Liberties. 277

full share of liberty, is a fact that must be recognized by those who have observed the course of events in England and the United States of America during this century.

The Greek idea that the State was the emanation of whatever exists in the nation of wisdom, light, and virtue, and consequently a civilizing agent, a modern instrument of progress, is the idea which modern liberals declare produced the immortal grandeur of Athens and the extraordinary fortune of Prussia. God's will, according to the Apostle St. Peter,[1] is:—

"Be ye subject therefore to every human creature for God's sake, whether it be to the king as excelling; or to governors as sent by him for the punishment of evil-doers and the praise of them that do well, for so is the will of God that by doing well you may put to silence the ignorance of foolish men : as free and not as making liberty a cloak for malice, but as the servants of God. Honour all men. Love the brotherhood. Fear God. Honour the king."

Historical Protestantism has shown itself incapable of carrying out the Divine maxims, and has been incapable of maintaining civil liberty. Without the aid of the secular arm it cannot even maintain itself as a general form of worship. Anti-Catholic or non-Catholic,

[1] 1st Epistle of St. Peter, chap. ii., verses 13 to 17.

civil liberty, such as the modern continental school of liberals are endeavouring to organize in the present day, will be as impotent as that which has gone before to stem the progress of the Universal Church.

CHAPTER IX.

CONCLUSION.

E read in the old missals of the Paris Liturgy, in the Introit of the Mass for Christmas Eve, the following passage :—

"Yet a little while and I shall shake the heavens, and the earth, and the sea, and the whole universe; I shall shake all the nations, and the Desired of all nations shall appear. Listen to this, ye peoples! Be attentive, O ye inhabitants of the earth."

The Jewish doctors, the learned and literary people of the time of Herod, were well acquainted with these words of Scripture, but they were indifferent to the great fact which took place in Bethlehem of Judæa.

The great men of the empire, with Cæsar at their head, had been warned by the Sibyl, but in vain. A few herdsmen of Judæa, a few fishermen of Galilee were more clear-sighted.

It was in the presence of a few shepherds assisting at the incarnation of the Light of the World—the greatest fact of the history of humanity—that the angels sang the following canticle, "*Gloria in excelsis Deo, et in terra pax hominibus bonæ voluntatis,*" "Glory to God in the highest, on earth peace to men of goodwill."

Let us frequently repeat it, and be thankful for the grace of Christian light; but let us not be proud, since that light comes to us not from ourselves but from on high.

Montesquieu, who had not seen it in his youth, made towards the end of his career, in the principal production of his science, matured by time and condensed by reflection, the following avowal:—

"An admirable thing is the Christian religion: it seems to have no other end in view than happiness in the next world, and yet it constitutes happiness in the present."[1]

Lord Macaulay states in disappointed tones that the Catholics who become Protestants are usually worthless, and the statement is decidedly correct; those who possess the faith once delivered to the saints remain Catholics, and those who lose it do not generally consider it worth while to profess any religion at all.

[1] "*Esprit des Lois,*" 24th, v. 3.

Catholic nations have received no promises of temporal riches nor of constant political success, but they have no cause for jealousy of other nations either in old or modern times.

When they have sought the kingdom of God and His justice, they know they will receive "over and above," according to the Divine word, all that prudent, wise, and reasonable men can desire.

The Catholic Church has been not only the foster-mother of all civilization for nearly 2,000 years, not only the sole depositary of Holy Writ and Christian truth in their integrity, but also the pure atmosphere in which human reason is preserved incorruptible and unshaken. Science, letters, and art were cultivated by her at a period when no one seemed to care for them, and when these Divine plants were even unknown by the rest of mankind.

The Catholic Church is even from a human point of view the grandest and most noble institution manifested to the world in the history of earthly things, and at this day the most solid and substantial. At every period of the history of the world it has shone forth resplendent by its faith and works, and its faithful disciples have walked in the first ranks, not only in the science of divinity but also in the human sciences.

Catholic nations are quite as well informed as others on the importance of capital and the value of labour, but they possess an admirable intermediary between these two sources of riches in the inexhaustible treasury of the Church, and if the economical development of our day is capable of being retained within bounds, certainly it will not find salvation elsewhere than in the bosom of the Church.

From St. Paul to St. Augustine, from St. Gregory of Nazianum to St. Thomas of Aquin, from Dante to Petrarch, from Roger Bacon to Corneille, from Descartes to Malebranche, from Bossuet to Châteaubriand, from Balmez to Newman, and from Lamartine to the ardent and noble youth that fill our schools, Catholic nations, invariable in the unity of their faith, have walked with firm and unerring step towards the conquest of the secrets of nature and created beauty.

Let their opponents rival them if they can, let them mount up the scale of human knowledge with them, let them multiply the applications of steam and electricity, let them analyze the properties of heat and explain the laws of light and penetrate the mystery of the composition of the sun.

They must go higher still.

Let them contemplate the unfathomable depths of

created space, and assist at the apparition (in our celestial sphere) of bodies whose light has travelled with prodigious rapidity towards it since the commencement of the world.

They must still go higher.

Let them resist if they can the admirable concert (called by the name of harmony) of the celestial bodies that bewilder our imagination.

Let them mount to those indefinite but created heights wherein is the region of fixed stars that approach the infinite. And when they have become wearied by study and rendered prostrate by the contemplation of these dazzling wonders, the Catholic may still cry, " Excelsior."

WORKS BY HIS EMINENCE CARDINAL MANNING.

ESSAYS ON RELIGION AND LITERATURE.
By Various Writers.

Demy 8vo., cloth, price 10s. 6d.

CONTENTS.—The Philosophy of Christianity—Mystic Elements of Religion—Controversy with the Agnostics—A Reasoning Thought—Darwinism brought to Book—Mr. Mill on Liberty of the Press—Christianity in relation to Society—The Religious Condition of Germany—The Philosophy of Bacon—Catholic Laymen and Scholastic Philosophy.

"There is great variety in style and treatment, and we should think the contents of the volume will be highly interesting to many who study such profound subjects."—*Edinburgh Courant.*

THE TRUE STORY OF THE VATICAN COUNCIL.

Crown 8vo., cloth, price 5s.

"A most valuable book of reference in the perpetually renewed controversies that have been raging for the last seven years."—*Tablet.*

"In Cardinal Manning's little volume he gives his story of the Council in clear, idiomatic English, and with the apparent conviction that the divisions produced in the Roman Catholic Church by the Council are of no moment, and that all will tend to the furtherance of his cause."—*Freeman.*

THE INDEPENDENCE OF THE HOLY SEE,

WITH AN APPENDIX CONTAINING THE PAPAL ALLOCUTION AND A TRANSLATION.

Crown 8vo., cloth, price 5s.

"Our hope is that the volume will get into the widest circulation. . . . The four discourses compacted together in this small volume barely exceed one hundred pages. They may be read with ease at a single sitting. They state, in the simplest manner possible, facts which are part and parcel of the world's history, and in marshalling these facts, they demonstrate, with the clearness of a syllogism, that the independence of the Holy See is as the keystone to the arch of good government in Christendom."—*Catholic Standard.*

C. KEGAN PAUL & CO., 1, PATERNOSTER SQUARE, LONDON.

WORKS BY AUBREY DE VERE.

ANTAR AND ZARA: an Eastern Romance.

INISFAIL, AND OTHER POEMS, MEDITATIVE AND LYRICAL.

Fcap. 8vo., price 6s.

"Mr. Aubrey De Vere is a charming poet, but if he were not so charming, he would still deserve signal recognition for the fact that he is entirely original; he stands alone, apart from other modern poets, unaffected by their work, and wholly without tinge of their mannerisms."—*Examiner.*

"Marked throughout by that high, pure tone of thought and expression which graces and dignifies his earliest as well as his later poems."—*Standard.*

THE FALL OF RORA,

THE SEARCH AFTER PROSERPINE, AND OTHER POEMS, MEDITATIVE AND LYRICAL.

Fcap. 8vo., price 6s.

"Mr. Aubrey De Vere's poems will always receive a warm welcome from a wide circle of cultivated readers."—*Morning Post.*

"There is, as is well known, always thought and lyrical facility in Mr. De Vere's verses, and many of these familiar pieces will be welcomed by their admirers."—*Graphic.*

"Graceful, polished, musical, and intensely imbued with classic spirit, which the author has since somewhat outgrown, many of the lyrics, sonnets, and longer poems in this volume are deserving of a permanent place in our literature."—*Scotsman.*

THE LEGENDS OF ST. PATRICK,

AND OTHER POEMS.

Small Crown 8vo., cloth, price 5s.

"Mr. De Vere's versification in his earlier poems is characterized by great sweetness and simplicity. He is master of his instrument, and rarely offends the ear with false notes."—*Pall Mall Gazette.*

"We have but space to commend the varied structure of his verse, the carefulness of his grammar, and his excellent English."—*Saturday Review.*

C. KEGAN PAUL & CO., 1, PATERNOSTER SQUARE, LONDON.

WORKS BY AUBREY DE VERE (*continued*).

THE INFANT BRIDAL AND OTHER POEMS.
A New and Enlarged Edition.
Fcap. 8vo., cloth, price 7s. 6d.

" A melancholy thoughtfulness is the leading characteristic of Mr. De Vere's writings, and it is a characteristic which will have a charm for very many minds."—*Glasgow News.*

" Whole passages are written with the earnest enthusiasm of an ardent scholar and thinker."—*Academy.*

ST. THOMAS OF CANTERBURY.
A Dramatic Poem.
Large Fcap. 8vo., cloth, price 5s.

" As a play it abounds in vigorous characterization. As a poem, in passages of so fine a strain of dignity and pathos as even to exalt a lofty theme."—*Daily News.*

" Interesting throughout. . . . Always melodious. . . . It is plainly the work of one who though a Catholic is liberal, and is a scholar and a gentleman."—*Academy.*

ALEXANDER THE GREAT.
A Dramatic Poem.
Small Crown 8vo., cloth, price 5s.

" In some points Mr. De Vere's poetry is a model to most of his fellow singers. Its idioms and phraseology are English, thorough and correct English; his verses, with few exceptions, are symmetrical, simple, and sweet; and his diction throughout is dignified, as becomes the stately muse of tragedy, and often rises to sublime pitch, leaving all his contemporaries far behind."—*Standard.*

" A noble play. . . . The work of a true poet and of a fine artist, in whom there is nothing vulgar and nothing weak. . . . We had no conception, from our knowledge of Mr. De Vere's former poems, that so much poetic power lay in him as this drama shows. It is terse as well as full of beauty, nervous as well as rich in thought."—*Spectator.*

C. KEGAN PAUL & CO., 1, PATERNOSTER SQUARE, LONDON.

THE CIVILIZATION OF THE PERIOD OF THE RENAISSANCE IN ITALY,

BY JACOB BURCKHARDT.

AUTHORIZED TRANSLATION BY S. G. C. MIDDLEMORE.

2 vols. Demy 8vo., cloth, 24s.

THE RENAISSANCE OF ART IN FRANCE,

BY MRS. MARK PATTISON.

With Illustrations. Demy 8vo., cloth. [*In Preparation.*]

CHARACTERISTICS FROM THE WRITINGS OF JOHN HENRY NEWMAN, D.D.

Being Selections, Personal, Historical, Philosophical, and Religious, from his various Works. Arranged with the Author's personal approval. Second Edition. With Portrait. Crown 8vo., cloth, price 6s.

Dr. Newman's mind is here presented in his own words on the great religious questions which have so largely exercised the intellect of this age, and which, even in the judgment of those who are unable to accept his conclusions, he has faced, investigated, and determined for himself, with an unflinching courage and an unswerving steadfastness of purpose almost as rare, perhaps, as the high mental endowments which he has brought to the task.

"Dr. Newman is a poet as well as a theologian, and this poetical feeling, combined with great sensitiveness and tenderness, as well as his mastery of the English language, give to all he writes a charm of which even his most thorough-going antagonists cannot fail to be sensible."—*Pall Mall Gazette.*

*** *A Portrait of Dr. J. H. Newman, mounted for framing, can be had, price 2s. 6d.*

C. KEGAN PAUL & CO., 1, PATERNOSTER SQUARE, LONDON.